The Scented Kitchen

FRANCES BISSELL is the author of many books and was *The Times'* food writer for thirteen years. Her articles have appeared in numerous publications in Britain, and she has been widely featured in the international press, including *The New York Times*, *San Francisco Examiner*, *Boston Globe*, *Le Figaro*, *Bangkok Post* and *El Diario de Jerez*, and magazines such as *Taste*, *A la Carte*, *Victoria* and *Food Arts*. She has written and presented two television series based in the West Country and appeared on a variety of TV shows in North America.

She has received the Glenfiddich Award for Cookery Writer of the Year in Britain, while her *Book of Food* won a James Beard Foundation Award in America. Frances Bissell has been guest chef in some of the world's leading hotels and restaurants, including the Café Royal Grill Room in London, the Mandarin Oriental in Hong Kong, the George V in Paris and The Mark in New York.

By the same author

The Scented Kitchen

Cooking
with flowers

Frances Bissell

To Rhicin
happy cooking
all good wishes
Frances Bissell

Serif
London

First published 2007 by
Serif
47 Strahan Road
London E3 5DA

9 8 7 6 5 4 3 2 1

British Library Cataloguing in Publication Data.
A catalogue record for this book is available from the British Library.

Library of Congress Cataloging-in-Publication Data.
A catalog record for this book is available from the Library of Congress.

ISBN 13: 978 1 897959 44 2
ISBN 10: 1 897959 44 3

Design, typesetting and photography by Sue Lamble

Printed and bound in Malaysia by Forum

Contents

In celebration of my parents'
Diamond Wedding Anniversary
2 June 1945 – 2 June 2005

and in memoriam RM
12 November 2006

Preface

For many years I have wanted to write about the cooking I do with flowers, but I haven't used the term 'edible flowers' in this book's sub-title. There are many flowers that are edible, which is to say they are not poisonous, and there are many edible flowers that are a pleasure to look at. However most of these edible flowers have a bland flavour vaguely reminiscent of green beans, pea pods or lettuce. This book is not about identifying and eating as many different flowers as possible or adding as many differently coloured petals as possible to a salad. It is primarily about using the flower's scent as a flavouring component, as one might use a herb or a spice.

A temperate climate, a love of flower gardens and a predilection for foraging for wild – and free – food provided me with the perfect conditions for exploring this intriguing and rewarding aspect of cooking. I began to use flowers in the kitchen during the hot summer of 1976. My parents' garden had a huge lavender bush with the deepest, most piercing fragrance imaginable. I often looked at that bush, wondering how I might capture its scent in my cooking. Tarragon vinegar was much in vogue at the time, so I infused a bottle of white wine vinegar with a bundle of lavender heads and was thrilled at the way the flowers' colour and scent were gradually released into the vinegar. Lavender sugar, syrups and sorbets soon followed, and I continued to cook with flowers whenever I could lay my hands on fragrant specimens, moving from lavender to roses, jasmine, violets, pinks and other blossoms.

'The use of herbs,' Elizabeth David wrote, 'is very much a matter of association, taste and prejudice.' I feel the same about the use of flowers in the kitchen. I do not expect everyone to like the flavour and scent of lavender as much as I do, but I hope that the recipes in that chapter will inspire readers to develop recipes to their own taste. On the other hand, if you enjoy rosemary, savory and hyssop, you will very probably like the flavour of lamb cooked with lavender.

The great majority of the recipes in this collection are of my own devising, and others, appropriately annotated, are based on the work of other cooks, some of whom have gone before me, some still living, who have also appreciated the unique contribution that flowers can make to a dish or a meal.

Disclaimer

Whilst the author and publisher have taken all reasonable steps to check the accuracy of the information in this book concerning the edibility of flowers used in the recipes, readers are strongly advised to carry out their own research if using flowers *not* mentioned in this book.

The author has consulted the National Poisons Information Service and has used as a guide *Poisonous Plants and Fungi* by Marion Cooper, Anthony Johnson and Elizabeth Dauncey, published in 2003 by the Stationery Office, the most accurate and up-to-date guide, in book form, at the time of writing, which she has found to be invaluable. She hereby acknowledges the work of these three specialists as an important source of information. The National Poisons Information Service has also contributed to the compilation of a CD developed by the Royal Botanic Gardens, Kew, which has been produced for doctors and other specialists.

Readers outside Britain are advised to consult their local, regional or state poison information authority for the most up-to-date guide available.

Neither the author nor the publisher can be held responsible for any accident whatsoever which may occur as a result of using this book.

Acknowledgements

Whenever we stayed with our friend Julia, she always wanted to know what I was working on, full of enthusiasm for my various projects. Last time we visited her in California, I told her that I was writing a book on cooking with flowers. 'Hmmm,' she said with a frown, 'What's it really about?' I explained that it was about extracting flower scents to add a new flavour dimension to use in the way we use herbs and spices. 'Well, that sounds really interesting and new,' she said, 'but you'd better think of another title. I wouldn't buy a book called "Cooking with Flowers".' Choosing a title that captures the essence of the book has been the hardest part. But enlightenment came one evening when I served my rose petal kulfi to our dinner guests. They sampled it, puzzled. Then one turned to the other with an astonished smile, saying, 'It tastes like the scent of roses.' Having decided on the title, I wrote to Julia. Her postcard, dated 5 August 2004, included the words, 'Your book title sounds perfect, and I can't wait to see it in print.' That was not to be, as she died a week later. I owe huge gratitude to her, for one does not lightly turn down advice from Julia Child.

And just as Julia and our dinner guests grasped what it was all about, so too did Stephen Hayward at Serif, and I am very glad that he wanted to publish a book that I have been working on for so long. I always knew that one day I would find a publisher who would understand the appeal of this esoteric branch of cookery and I am very grateful to Stephen and also to Sue Lamble and to Justus Oehler for the care they have taken to produce such a handsome book.

Margaret and Graeme Andrews, Julian Barnes and Pat Kavanagh, Alison Bolton, Fiona and Desmond Hayward, Mona Howard, Sylvia and Michael Jay, Clare and James Kirkman, Bob and Mary Maloney, Paul Levy and Penelope Marcus, Nick and Jane Mavrikakis, Margaret and Henry Minto, Pat and Herbert Pratt, Alison and James Riddell, Kiran and Jeremy Sandford, Caroline and Patrick Taylor are amongst those who, over the years, have given me flowers from their gardens or access to their kitchens, sometimes both. I am grateful to them all, and to any whom I have forgotten to name. I am especially grateful to Jane Ellis, Curator, and Danny Snapes, Head Gardener, at the National Trust's Fenton House in Hampstead for providing me with flowers for testing many of my recipes, and for also giving me the opportunity to show others how to cook with flowers at various open days held in the gardens of Fenton House.

Tom Bissell has tasted and eaten his way through flower jellies and syrups, exotic cocktails and countless rose and lavender recipes without a murmur. As always, he has my love and gratitude, for his enthusiasm, support, encouragement and boundless love.

A brief and partial history of the scented kitchen

'Here's flowers for you;
Hot lavender, mints, savory, marjoram:
The marigold, that goes to bed wi' the sun.'
William Shakespeare, *The Winter's Tale*

I have vivid memories of a vegetarian lunch in California in the early 1980s. A white bean soup was followed by a wild mushroom risotto and then a gratin of celeriac. But the last dish was the star of the show, a salad of tiny leaves and flowers, including rose petals, borage flowers, marigold petals and wild pansies, or heartsease, called Johnny Jump-ups in North America. It looked and smelled divine, a shower of fragrant, colourful confetti among the bright green leaves. There is a long tradition of using flowers in the kitchen, and in eating that salad we were wandering down one of the more intriguing by-ways of culinary history. That lunch with Alice Waters at Chez Panisse in Berkeley was an experience to be added to that of my parents' lavender-filled garden and another flower recipe joined my collection, out of which this book has grown.

Apicius' *De re coquinaria*, the most important surviving document on Roman culinary practices, describes how Roman cooks flavoured wine with roses and violets and sweetened it with a little honey before serving. In the first century AD the Greek botanist and physician Dioscorides proposed an infusion made from lavender flowers. Even then, lavender was known as a source of well-being and Dioscorides may well have been suggesting it for medicinal rather than gastronomic purposes, for lavender has long been used as a herbal remedy.

Flowers were widely used in medieval cooking, not only in England, but also in France and Italy, where this might be attributed to Roman influences. In Iberia and in the eastern Mediterranean, the use of orange flower water and of rosewater was a practice introduced during the lengthy period of Muslim occupation. As early as the fourth century BC, the Egyptians had perfected the art of distilling in order to make turpentine, and the Arabs later employed the same technique to extract oil of roses and oil of orange flowers, of which the scented flower waters were a by-product.

Documents show that mixed herb and flower salads using borage, daisies, primroses and violets were enjoyed in England as long ago as the fifteenth century, and the fashion continued throughout the Tudor and Stuart periods. By the middle of the seventeenth century, flowers were an important ingredient in the English kitchen as well as in the still-room. *Gerard's Herball* of 1597 warns against the over-use of such potently flavoured mixtures by 'some unlearned physitians and divers rash and overbold apothecaries, and other foolish women', for these were, of course, used as medicine. Lavender, mixed with cinnamon, nutmegs and cloves, 'made into a powder, and given to drinke in the distilled water thereof, doth helpe the panting and passion of the heart', according to Gerard. *A Book of Fruits and Flowers*, dated 1653, a collection of household recipes, some of them from the late sixteenth century, commissioned and possibly collected by Thomas Jenner, has recipes for syrups and conserves of roses, violets and cowslips.

One of the richest sources for dishes involving flowers is *The Queen's Closet Opened*, a trilogy published in 1655 and said to have been transcribed from the recipe books of the exiled Queen Henrietta Maria. Rosewater was used in making Banbury cakes, Shrewsbury cakes, a delicate rice cream and 'a very good great Oxfordshire cake' requiring three pounds of butter, sixteen eggs and half a pint of rosewater. The cake's glazing of egg white, sugar and rosewater is also very nice. Fine pies 'after the French fashion' had a filling of veal, beef suet, raisins, currants, dates, prunes, spices, verjuice and rosewater, and sound remarkably similar to the original mince pies, which, of course, had meat in them. A classic recipe for elderflower vinegar is to be found here, as well as one for pickling broom buds. And the gooseberry fool recipe includes rosewater, a nice touch that I often include when I make this classic summer dish. The recipe for 'Pyramidis Cream' is very similar to *panna cotta*, perhaps even nicer, combining gelatine and cream with a flavouring of rosewater and pounded almonds. Eels are cooked with a white wine, herb and saffron sauce. Poor Knights, a dish of bread slices dipped in egg and fried, something like *pain perdu* or French toast, are served with rosewater, sugar and butter. Syrup of clove gilly flowers, two recipes for rose petal conserve, one cooked, one uncooked, and lozenges of red roses, are some of the methods given for preserving the flower's fleeting fragrance.

Detailed instructions are given for flower conserves, including one for violets 'in the Italian Manner' in which the petals are simply pounded with twice their weight in sugar; similarly borage flowers, which require three times their weight, and rosemary flowers, made with equal quantities of flowers and sugar. Sage flowers, peonies and lavender are made into conserves, all with three times their weight in sugar. These conserves seem to have been prescribed as tonics and cordials rather than used for strictly culinary purposes. The recipes for candied flowers are very useable, as is that for rose petal sugar, in which the rose petals are first dried in the oven and then beaten to a powder.

My favourite recipe in *The Queen's Closet* is for a marbled flower paste that encapsulates what this book is all about, the scent of flowers captured as a flavour:

To make Paste of flowers of the colour of Marble, tasting of natural flowers.

Take every sort of pleasing Flowers, as Violets, Cowslips, Gilly-flowers, Roses or Marigolds, and beat them in a mortar, each flower by itself with sugar, until the sugar become the colour of the flower, then put a little Gum Dragon steept in water into it, and beat it into a perfect paste; and when you have half a dozen colours, every flower will take of its nature, then rowl the paste therein, and lay one piece upon another, in mingling sort, so rowl your Paste in small rowls, as big and as long as your finger, then cut it off the bigness of a small nut, overthwart, and so rowl them thin, that you may see a knife through them, so dry them before the fire till they be dry.

A bit of a mouthful to read in one extended sentence, but so vivid in its instructions. Gum Dragon is powdered tragacanth, a useful ingredient when working with flowers, more details of which are given on p.41. John Evelyn's *Acetaria* of 1699 recommends certain flowers to be eaten with 'other salleting', very like today's flower-strewn salads, and as a 'more palatable relish' he also suggests infusing clove gillyflowers, elderflowers, orange blossom and cowslips in vinegar. His recipe for 'Taffata tarts' is not as elaborate, or as delicious, it has to be said, as that in *The Queen's Closet*, on which I have based the recipe on p.163. The two books have almost identical recipes for veal jelly, even down to the subtle touch of putting a few sprigs of rosemary in the bottom of the jelly bag before letting the liquid drip through. Evelyn also adds the zest of a lemon, which gives the merest zephyr of a citrus flavour to the jelly. Robert May, the 'accomplish't Cook' of the great English and French houses of the seventeenth century, has many recipes similar to those of his contemporaries. 'To make almond bisket' he includes rosewater with the almonds, 'to keep them from oiling', and several other almond-based recipes also employ rosewater. He uses saffron in 'Tortelleti, or little pasties'. May's many recipes for 'grand sallets' include borage, ransoms, clove carnations, cowslips, primroses, violets. He has recipes for both rose and elderflower vinegar, and others for possets, creams and 'blancmanger' that use flower flavouring, usually rosewater, and he also gives instructions for pickling and candying flowers.

Elinor Fettiplace, the 'grande dame' of the Elizabethan kitchen and household, used rosewater in both sweet and savoury dishes, the most appealing of which is her rabbit pie, served hot with a caudle. This is a very good way of preparing pies, whether meat or fruit. The pie filling is baked under its crust in the usual way and, about half an hour before it is done, egg yolk, cream, spices and rosewater are beaten together and carefully poured into the pie by means of a funnel which is inserted through the centre of the crust. It is then returned to the oven for 30 minutes for the caudle to seep into and enrich the pie filling.

Hilary Spurling speculates that in the seventeenth century roses must have been grown on what almost amounted to a commercial scale in the gardens of some England's grand houses. A contemporary recipe for rose syrup, for example, called for eleven gallons of rose petals, for which an acre of roses would be required.

Giacomo Castelvetro, a much-travelled nobleman from Modena and a frequent visitor to aristocratic houses in England and Scotland during the late sixteenth and early seventeenth centuries, wrote on gardening and cooking amongst other subjects, and his writings include details of salads with flowers as well as strict instructions on how to dress them, as he despaired of the English habit of drowning salads in vinegar. I used to visit friends near Modena who had a restaurant in which they served Castelvetro's salad, with busy lizzie flowers, nasturtiums, violas and whatever else was in season in their organic garden. Extra virgin olive oil from nearby Brisighella and the family's own very fine *aceto balsamico tradizionale de Modena* were the only condiments allowed on this exquisite salad apart from a crunch of sea salt and a little freshly ground pepper.

Like many of her eighteenth-century contemporaries, Hannah Glasse makes ample use of flowers and flower essences in her book. Desserts involving almonds, for example, almost always include orange flower water or rosewater, or sometimes both. Conserve of red roses, syrup of clove gillyflowers, syrup of peach blossom and syrup of roses are to be found, as are instructions 'to candy any sort of flowers' and for saffron cheesecake. My favourite is the recipe for 'fairy butter', partly because of its name, and I have included it on p.141. Fairy butter does very nicely at a summer tea party, especially if you cannot obtain clotted cream for your scones. Mrs Glasse's almond custards are flavoured with rosewater and her macaroons with orange flower water. Although she does not give a recipe for syrup of violets, several of her recipes use it for colouring jellies and creams, but her readers could have found a recipe in the *Cooks and Confectioners Dictionary* by her contemporary John Nott.

And then we come to the Victorians, Miss Acton, Mrs Beeton, Mrs Marshall and their contemporaries. It puzzles me that claims are constantly made that cooking with flowers was an important part of the Victorian kitchen, as there is almost no evidence to support them.

Miss Acton herself puzzles me. She is a very early nineteenth-century lady, and one might have expected some lingering overtones of eighteenth-century cookery in her writing, for example using flower scents and flavours in desserts, and capturing them in preserves, jellies and wines. But the more one reads her, the more one gets the sense of a very modern woman, writing for her peers, who had no time for the still-room or for gathering wild flowers. She lived at the dawn of the industrial age when both men and women were beginning to lead busy lives outside the home and she set out to help the housewife or cook to produce straightforward, wholesome food. Her almond macaroons have no flower water, nor do her gooseberry recipes mention elderflower. Her use of flowers appears to be confined to a suggestion of orange flower water or vanilla in her recipe for French Custards or Creams and a most unusual recipe for orange flower macaroons in which snipped up fresh blossoms are mixed with powdered sugar and folded into beaten egg whites before being baked. One wonders where the English cook – then or now – was supposed to find large quantities of orange blossom. Her dessert recipes are all rather elegant and one might expect to find in them the extra dimension that flowers give to the flavour of food, but perhaps this was something she simply did not enjoy.

I use the 1899 edition of Mrs Beeton's *Household Management*, from which, it is claimed, 'none of the recipes have been taken away'. It virtually ignores the use of flowers and flower essences in the kitchen and the author emerges as a thoroughly urban, modern woman who can't be bothered with rustic ways. But perhaps she was also being realistic, tacitly acknowledging that the middle classes often lived in the new mansion flats of the period and did not have access to gardens. It cannot be that she wanted to do away with elaborate confections, as she has plenty of recipes for preserves and pickles and an extraordinary collection of recipes for elaborate pastry and sugar work centrepieces illustrated with drawings that might have come from an architect's studio. Perhaps she was simply reflecting the taste of the time in which she lived.

Mrs Beeton does suggest nasturtiums as a garnish for her summer salad. In fact, she has very few salad recipes, limited to winter, summer, cucumber, potato and red cabbage, so there are none of those deliciously baroque confections of the eighteenth century, which in turn are reminiscent of those of the seventeenth century, like Joan Cromwell's Grand Sallets.

Mrs Agnes Marshall, who wrote towards the end of the nineteenth century, was famous for her ice-creams, her cooking school, her lecture tours and her commercial products, made limited use of flowers in her ice-cream recipes, which include rosewater ice, using fresh petals, jasmine ice water, using essence of jasmine, and a very appealing orange flower water ice-cream made with almonds, cream, sugar, egg yolks and, of course, orange flower water.

Further evidence of the Victorians' lack of interest in using flowers in the kitchen is provided by a study of manuscript household receipt books of the sort one comes across in county archives. In Birmingham Central Library, for example, there is a collection of small notebooks, written between 1779 and 1883 by local ladies, including Maria Fairfax, daughter of John Cadbury. She was born in 1838, married in 1881 and started her collection of 'Sundry Useful Recipes' in 1883. There is also a recipe book written a generation earlier by Candida Cadbury, who was probably Maria's mother. Constance Hadon began writing down her recipes in 1858 and Anne Taylor in 1857, and there are such strong similarities, including the handwriting as well as the recipes, between their books, that I suspect that they were sisters. Many of the recipes are almost identical to those recorded by Sarah Wye, writing almost a century earlier, and my guess is that all these women were either related or came from the same social circle. There is, for example, a recipe for 'chutnee' common to most of them, and another for a similar condiment, Tapp sauce. If cooking with flowers had been part of the Victorian repertoire, these manuscripts and others like them would be exactly where one would expect to find the recipes, but there is nothing.

It would also seem that using flowers in the kitchen did not commend itself greatly to colonial cooks of the Victorian period. Caroline Sullivan, author of *The Jamaica Cookery Book*, published in Kingston in 1893, uses rosewater in a few desserts, but makes no mention of native flowers. This could, of course, be because she, like most European settlers in tropical and sub-tropical climates, did not know which indigenous plants were edible and which were poisonous. On the other hand, Hildagonda Duckitt, the great South African cook and housekeeper, waxes lyrical about native Cape flowers, as well as the abundance of violets and stocks in her own garden in December. We also learn from her that strawberries and violets were a source of income on farms in the Stellenbosch neighbourhood – but, irritatingly, she does not explain what the violets were used for. All the ingredients for exquisite flower recipes were certainly available in 1900, for she describes how to make a pot-pourri using rose petals, jasmine, orange blossoms, lavender and myrtle amongst other things, but it does not appear that any of these ingredients were used in the kitchen. We can only conclude that the violets were simply sold as bunches of flowers in the market at Cape Town.

When I lived in the Cape in the early 1960s, I tasted nothing to indicate that flowers were used in the kitchen. The only exception was the Cape Malay use of both rosewater and saffron, which comes as no great surprise when one remembers that community's Muslim heritage. There are several sago-based puddings that are scented with rosewater, including boerboer, also flavoured with cardamom and cinnamon and sent round to friends and neighbours as a gift half-way through Ramadan.

American sources quote Dolley Madison, an early nineteenth-century First Lady, as having used a recipe for Fairy Butter, the delicate and pretty confection flavoured with orange flower water, which was said to be popular among Virginia housewives of the time. The recipe was almost certainly taken from an English cookbook, as Dolley Madison was descended from English Quakers who settled in Virginia early in the eighteenth century.

Harriott Pinckney Horry, an eighteenth-century heiress living on a South Carolina plantation, recorded a number of recipes using flowers in the English fashion. One is for a large quantity of orange flower syrup, using nine pounds of sugar and half a pound of flowers. She also makes a rather good orange flower ratafia in which a pound of flowers, an ounce of ground cinnamon, two ounces of peach kernels, a pound of sugar and a quart of cold water are mixed with a gallon of 'French-Brandy in a Jug to Ferment for a Month, taking Care to Shake it once or twice a Day'. Her recipe for 'Mackaroons' is almost identical to that found in eighteenth-century recipe books published in England, pounding the ground almonds with rosewater, while she uses orange flower water to flavour her cheesecake.

It is not until the 1930s, when Eleanour Sinclair Rohde and

Florence White were writing, and the 1940s and '50s, when the gardener-cooks Nell Heaton and Constance Spry were active, that we see renewed interest in flowers as food in England. These women were writing for a public that was not necessarily based in the country, but for middle-class readers with their own gardens and, quite possibly, gardeners.

There is, however, every indication that, even though the Victorian cookery writers virtually ignored the use of flowers in the kitchen, it was a rural foodway that had never disappeared. Dorothy Hartley, who was writing in the 1950s but based her books on her much earlier experiences as a cook, researcher and teacher in the 1920s and '30s, has recipes for candied cowslips, cowslip wine, rose petal jam, marigold cheese and marigold salad, dandelion wine and coltsfoot wine, ingredients more easily available to the country dweller than those living in towns and cities.

Women's Institute publications are a rich source of information about contemporary rural cooking and *The Country Housewife's Handbook*, compiled by the West Kent Federation of Women's Institutes in 1939, reprinted several times and with new editions in 1943 and 1948, is no exception. Even at a time of great privation, traditional recipes including rose petal vinegar, a syrup of violets not very different from John Nott's eighteenth-century recipe, violet vinegar, elderflower champagne, elderflower wine, dandelion wine and rose petal wine were still being recorded.

The recipe for rose petal wine in the 1948 edition is notably laconic – the author and editors assumed that readers would be familiar with recipes of this sort and there are strong indications that in the country they were always current, handed down from generation to generation.

> To every pint of rose petals, of any colour, add 1 quart boiling water. Stir well and press. Strain and pour 1/2 pint more water over petals. Strain again and to every quart of liquid add 1 lb sugar and boil for 20 minutes. When cool, set to work with 1 oz yeast. When finished working, bottle off. This wine improves with keeping, so give it a fair chance and add more sugar if needed when 3 months old.

Most of all, I like 'Essential Oil of Flowers and Herbs – Great-Grandmother's Way of Scenting Her Clothes' Chest and Drawers':

> Steep some cotton wool or wadding in some pure olive oil. Put a layer of it in an earthenware jar. Cover with a thick layer of

fresh rose leaves, carnations, pinks, jasmine, wallflowers, magnolia blossoms, tuberose or any other flower you wish to obtain the perfume. Spread over the flowers another layer of the cotton wool steeped in oil and more flowers. Repeat until the jar is full. Cover closely and stand in the sun for a week. Then throw away flowers, carefully press out the oil from the cotton wool and put into a bottle for use. The oil will have imbibed the odour of the flowers. The cotton wool will perfume your chests and drawers.

This is a simple adaptation of the perfumer's technique of *enfleurage* and it is very effective. There are also instructions for making lavender sugar in the same way as rosemary sugar, putting sprigs in a jar of sugar and leaving it for a week. 'This flavoured sugar is unusual, and good with any milk sweet.'

Country recipe collections continued to reflect the interest in flowers in the 1970s, for example, with recipes for hawthorn liqueur, dandelion wine, elderflower champagne and elderflower fritters. *The Gentle Art of Cookery* by Mrs C. F. Leyel and Miss Olga Hartley, first published in 1925, was reissued in the early 1980s. Mrs Leyel was a founder of the Society of Herbalists and also of Culpeper, the herbal shop, but despite these qualifications some of the information in the book is dangerously misleading. The authors claim, for example, that the Chinese produce a tea scented with oleander flowers. This cannot be – oleander is one of the most poisonous plants known to science. Deaths have been recorded following the eating of kebabs grilled on oleander twigs and it is said to be dangerous even to rest or fall asleep under an oleander bush. But I do like the sound of her primrose vinegar, and also of her 'ice-cream of roses' using rose-infused cream as the base. She recommends Marcel Boulestin's omelette made with yellow salsify flowers, which, she says, are delicious. A mixture of marigolds and nasturtiums makes a nice omelette filling in the absence of salsify flowers.

Cowslip pudding, daisy wine, cowslip wine and dandelion wine and a lengthy, complex and rather expensive recipe for marigold cordial are all included. Many of these are traditional English recipes, but the book also has a nice use of chrysanthemum petals, blanched first in salted and acidulated water and then mixed with potatoes, artichoke hearts, shrimps and capers. I have included a modern version in the relevant chapter, as we can now buy excellent crayfish tails in brine.

Another classic reissued in the 1980s, Mrs Leyel's *Herbal Delights*, should be used with a degree of caution, bearing in mind that it was last revised in 1947, when there was much less information available than there is now. She writes of the sweet pea, for example, that 'generally speaking the plants of this order are poisonous' and then goes on to write, 'Sweet peas can be used in salads as decorations, and can be eaten.' Confused? I certainly am, so, regrettably, I have omitted them from this book.

Elizabeth David's *Spices, Salt and Aromatics in the English Kitchen*, first published in 1970, makes almost no mention of the use of flowers as aromatics, with the exception of Marigold Cheese, which is based on the recipe from Mrs Leyel's *Herbal Delights*. It is essentially a junket, made with good milk, rennet and the juice of pounded marigold petals. The curdled mixture is eventually spooned into a jelly bag and, once the whey has run out, the curds are packed into a mould and then pressed under a weight.

Although I have described this chapter as a brief history of cooking with flowers, there are geographical and other factors that have also helped determine which culinary cultures make use of scented flowers and which do not.

For centuries England has been in the fortunate position of benefiting both from what it can grow and also from what it imports. Roses, unlike oranges, grow well in our climate and rosewater has long been made here, but even the briefest survey of old English recipe books indicates that large quantities of orange flower water were imported.

It is tempting to argue that the boundary between the lands where orange flower water is used in preference to rosewater is almost as distinctive as that between olive and animal fats in cooking, but it is not quite that simple. Rosewater came from Persia and spread to India with the subcontinent's Moghul invaders, and also through Turkey into the Balkans. Orange trees passed from China via the Arabs to the Mediterranean, North Africa and Iberia. This picture is, of course, a simplified one, for there is some overlap between the two flower waters, but as a rule of thumb one can say that rosewater is used in Persian, Indian and Turkish cookery, whereas orange flower water tends to be the scent used in Arabic cooking and its descendants, although scented flower waters are little used in contemporary Iberian cooking.

Some Middle Eastern recipes, like *muhallabiyeh*, a milk pudding made with ground rice, are flavoured with both rosewater and orange flower water. If the two flower waters are used together, more orange than rose should be used – a ratio of 4:1 is about right. The dish, once set, is garnished with chopped mixed nuts, almonds, peeled pistachios and walnuts. *Khoshaf* is the Lebanese version of a macerated dried fruit salad in which apricots and seedless raisins are flavoured with both orange flower and rosewater. The fruit is steeped overnight in water together with the flavourings and mixed nuts are then added before chilling and serving.

The rose remains a favourite flavouring in Persian and Indian sweets, such as *ras gula* and *gulab jamun*, in which either rosewater or the much more intense rose essence is used. Certain festive rice dishes will also be perfumed with rosewater, such as the wonderful *Shah Jahani biryani*, a dish in which subtly spiced chicken is layered with rose- and saffron-scented rice and cream and served with rose petals, crushed nuts and silver leaf scattered over the surface.

Sri Lanka has a wonderfully varied cuisine, with unfolding layers revealing the various cultural influences that have washed over the island throughout its history. Rosewater, rather than the orange flower water that one might expect, is used in desserts originating with the Portuguese colonisers of the seventeenth century. Alongside *bolo fiado* and Love Cake, native blooms such as plantain and banana flowers are used in rich pickles and piquant sambals.

Extensive travels in the Far East in the 1980s and '90s led me into many kitchens, but I found the use of flowers elusive in the extreme. On the whole, fragrance came from leaves and roots, not flowers, of ginger, pandanus, lemon grass and basil. Chrysanthemum petals and dried lily buds are to be found in soups in Japan and China and banana flowers in the Indonesian kitchen. Cabbage roses are said to be cooked and served whole in China, but I have never had an opportunity to try them. In the Philippines, on the other hand, saffron is used in some rice dishes, which are obviously Spanish in origin, while the Thais use flower fragrances to perfume desserts, especially those made with coconut milk. Rose petals, jasmine flowers and other fragrant blossoms are soaked overnight in water to obtain a very delicate fragrance and this water is combined with the coconut flesh to extract the milk. For the last 50 years there has been a Japanese lavender industry in Furano on the island of Hokkaido. Recently, as imports of lavender essence and products have become less expensive, the lavender fields have become primarily a tourist attraction, although some local chefs use the flower in their cooking.

Moroccan food is famous for its delicately perfumed dishes. Tagines are flavoured with *ras el hanout*, a spice mixture made to the secret recipe of the individual spice-seller that traditionally includes rose-buds and lavender. When I first went to Marrakech, Abdelatif, a sous-chef from our hotel, took me to the spice souk. It was a great advantage going with a culinary expert rather than with a tourist guide. Abdelatif knew all the spice merchants and their families, and we were courteously received in spice shops which are also medicine shops, where dried parts of animals, birds and reptiles and bundles of medicinal plants and bark hang above the sacks of cinnamon, cumin, saffron, ginger and various spice mixes.

In Morocco, orange flower water is used in the rich almond pastries or the syrups that are poured over them, and it is also used to flavour and perfume fresh fruit. Sweet and savoury flavours are combined in certain tagines, where fruit is added to the meat. Thus mutton with prunes or quinces, a rich panoply of spices, including saffron, will be finished off with a splash of orange flower water just before serving.

Since the seventeenth century, production of oil or attar of roses, of which rosewater is a by-product, has been centred on the rose-growing valley of Kazanlak in Bulgaria. Maria Kaneva-Johnson, a leading authority on Balkan cooking, gives a recipe for a rose petal preserve and another for a rather fine red sauce. I would have expected more, but perhaps attar of roses is too costly to be squandered on mere food. Austria seems to be the western border at which the use of roses in cooking stops, which is no surprise when one remembers that the Turks twice tried, and twice failed, to capture Vienna. Despite their name, *Rosenkrapfen* are not rose-flavoured but rose-shaped pastries.

Today, violets, roses and lavender are used in the French kitchen, especially by pastry chefs. Pierre Herme, for example, one of the world's finest *pâtissiers*, uses flowers in combination with fruit flavours in his exquisite *macarons*, violets with blackcurrant and roses with raspberries for example. Festivals to celebrate flowers and flower culture are to be found not only in France, but also in the United States, where everything from the humble dandelion to lavender has its champions.

Techniques, blueprint recipes and equipment

The key to most of the recipes in this book is capturing and then preserving a flower's flavour and scent. While flowers make a charming addition to salads – and I make a number of suggestions for these – I am more interested in extracting a flower's essence and, in some cases, its colour in order to add another dimension to a dish than in decorating a salad. How to achieve this is the subject of this chapter.

There are many techniques for preserving food and most, including pickling, drying and freezing, can be used in flower cookery. I have to admit that some techniques attract me less than others. Pickled broom and other flower buds were popular ingredients in the 'grand sallet' of the seventeenth century, but I am not fond enough of pickles to devote space to the idea beyond the recipe for carnation sauce as an accompaniment to lamb on p.54. Even when I gather capers – another edible flower bud – I do not pickle them, but preserve them in sea salt. As my interest in using flowers in the kitchen grew, I learned that, without going to the lengths of distillation and decoction, it is possible to borrow certain techniques from the perfumer's art, such as *enfleurage* and maceration.

With flower flavours I often use the same technique of layering that one uses with perfume. Before

'In April macerated broom and orange blossom, in May a sea of roses, the scent from which submerged the city in a creamy, invisible fog for a whole month… Jasmine season began at the end of July, August was for tube roses.'

Patrick Süskind, *Perfume*

spraying on a favourite scent, one might also use the
soap, body lotion and talc. Using the same principle,
I make a rose kulfi with powdered rose petals and
rosewater, and serve it with rose syrup. If I glaze a cold
fillet of salmon with elderflower jelly, I sometimes
accompany it with a salad dressed with elderflower
vinaigrette.

The following recipes are intended as blueprints,
reflecting all the basic techniques for extracting scents
and flavours, from preserving in acid, sugar and salt, to
desiccation, maceration and *enfleurage*.

Flower butters

This is where the technique known as *enfleurage* is
used. It is not difficult, but you do need plenty of
flower petals. All you do is wrap a piece of fresh,
unsalted butter in muslin, bury it in a bowl of petals,
cover and leave it in a cool place for about 12 hours.
Then unwrap the butter, which has become
'enflowered' or infused with the scent of the flower.
It is delicious on toast or tea-time scones. This
method works well with roses, jasmine, pinks and
violets, but not with lavender, which is too strong to
use in the quantities required.

Another way to make flower butter is simply to blend
unsalted butter with the flower of your choice, petals
only. You can then roll the butter in cling film, wrap it
tightly, freeze and simply cut off a slice when you
require it. This is the same method used for making
beurre maître d'hôtel with tarragon, chives and other
herbs, and the one I would recommend for lavender
butter, blending about a tablespoon of loosely packed
flowers with a 250 g/8 oz block of unsalted butter.

A tea sandwich recipe that came into vogue in the
1920s calls for rose petal butter spread on a slice cut
from a large tin loaf. The surface is then covered with
fresh rose petals, another slice of buttered bread is
placed on top, the crusts are removed and the

sandwich cut into fingers or triangles. An even nicer version, I have found, is to slice the tin loaf lengthways, butter it, spread rose petals over it, then roll the slice of bread, from the short side, as if it were a Swiss roll. You can keep this covered with a damp cloth and cling film until ready to serve, which you do by slicing into pinwheels.

Other flower butters, such as nasturtium and marigold, can be prepared using a blender to make these pinwheel sandwiches, which are transformed by their bright, peppery flavour and lively colour.

Flower custard

Here the technique used is infusion. The best flowers to use are elderflowers, roses, violets, jasmine and lavender. You will only need a teaspoon of lavender blooms for this quantity of cream and eggs, whereas a handful or two of the other flowers will be fine.

Put the cream in a saucepan with the flower petals and bring it gently to the boil. Mix the sugar and egg yolks in a bowl and pour on the scalded cream, stirring well. Pour back into the saucepan, add the essence, if using it, and simmer gently for a couple of minutes, stirring continuously. Do not to allow the custard to boil or it will curdle. Remove from the heat and allow to cool before refrigerating. Cover the surface with butter paper or cling film to prevent a skin from forming. Strain before serving or before using in a trifle or making ice-cream.

serves 4 to 6

600 ml / 1 pint cream
flower petals
125 g / generous 4 oz caster sugar
8 egg yolks
a drop of flower essence (optional)

Flower jellies

Small jars of prettily coloured jelly make ideal presents, but they are so delicious that it can be quite difficult to part with them. As with a flower syrup, the flower scent is transmuted into the most exquisite flavour and preserved by means of the sugar.

There are two ways to make these, one with apple extract as a base to provide the pectin, the other using jam sugar with the flower infusion. I use apples when making lavender and sometimes rose jelly, because of the deep fragrance, which still comes through the apple flavour. I also employ an apple base to make a savoury jelly, such as fennel flower and chilli jelly. With elderflowers, carnations and jasmine, however, I prefer to use jam sugar, because apples produce a jelly that ranges from pale pink to deep garnet, the pale flowers look better with a paler jelly; see the note on sugars on p.28.

If you make lavender jelly, the equivalent of one flower head per 400 g / 14 oz jar is sufficient, but you can add another sprig to each jar as decoration.

Lavender jelly

Most varieties of cooking apple are a good basis for this jelly. I particularly like Granny Smiths, but see the note on apples on p.42.

Wash the apples, cut them into chunks and put in a large saucepan. Cover with water and simmer until the apples are tender and pulpy. Strain the pulp through a jelly bag without squeezing or forcing, otherwise the jelly will be cloudy.

Measure the liquid and add 500 g / 1 lb of sugar for each 600 ml / 1 pint of liquid. Strain the lemon juice into a saucepan and add the apple juice and sugar together with 5 of the lavender sprigs tied in muslin or secured in a tea filter. Bring to the boil and cook

makes about 2 kg/4 lb

2 kg / 4 lb tart apples
10 sprigs of lavender
juice of 2 lemons
granulated or preserving sugar –
    see recipe

briskly for 10 minutes or until setting point is reached, which is when a drop of the syrup will set on a cold saucer.

Remove the lavender and pour the jelly into sterilised jars. Add an extra sprig of lavender to each jar for identification, seal and label.

Fennel flower and chilli jelly

This is fabulous with hot or cold ham and with pork dishes.

Prepare 500 ml / 18 fl oz of apple extract following the instructions for lavender jelly in the previous recipe.

Put all the ingredients in a saucepan, securing the chilli and fennel in muslin or a tea filter. Heat gently until the sugar has dissolved, then boil briskly until setting point has been reached. Remove the chilli and fennel, decant the jelly into small hot jars, seal and label. If you wish, you can add a piece of chilli and a fennel flower to the jar, both as decoration and also for easy identification.

makes about 500 g

500 ml / 18 fl oz apple extract
500 g / 18 oz granulated sugar
2 large heads of fennel flowers
1 small hot red chilli
juice of 1 lime

Cook's tip

Rosemary or sage flowers can be used in place of fennel flowers, and you can also make a stunning jelly of nasturtium flowers and chilli using the same method.

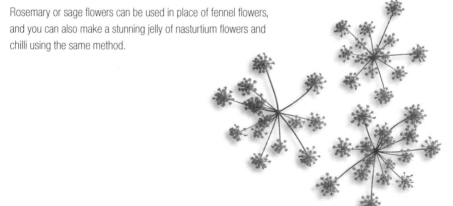

Flower oils

After reading Patrick Süskind's wonderful novel, *Perfume*, I began to experiment with culinary flower oils by means of the *enfleurage* technique. Instead of layering petals and cotton wool, saturating it in oil and then squeezing out the flower-infused oil, I simply filled a flask with flower petals, poured in oil and sealed it with the stopper. After leaving it for a few days, I strained the flowers out of the oil and repeated the exercise with fresh flowers.

Olive oil is not well suited for this purpose, because its flavour is too strong. I like to use grape seed oil, as it is pleasantly neutral. Groundnut oil is also suitable, while sunflower oil makes an inexpensive alternative.

Flower oils go brilliantly with shellfish. Imagine a lobster brushed with jasmine oil prior to being roasted, or perhaps rose or carnation oil brushed on scallops before you grill them. Lavender oil is good brushed on vegetables such as peppers and aubergines before roasting them. However flavouring oil with lavender needs only three or four flower heads for a litre bottle of oil, and to make this I simply open a fresh bottle of oil, slip in the flowers and re-cork.

Flower oil for immediate use can also be made by blending the petals with oil, almost as if you were making a pesto. This is the method I use for nasturtium or marigold oil and also for a brilliant blue borage flower oil (p.84).

Flower sugars

These can be stored in airtight containers kept in a dark place and will retain their flavour for about a year, until the flower season comes round again.

You will want to experiment with proportions depending on which flowers you are using – lavender, for example, will scent a larger amount of sugar than jasmine. Generally speaking, I make rose, lavender and sometimes rosemary flower and carnation sugars, preferring to preserve the flavour of flowers such as elderflowers and jasmine as syrups and jellies.

Even if you have only a small quantity of flowers, a couple of roses or half a dozen sprigs of lavender, it is still worth flavouring some sugar. I keep it in empty spice jars, along with my vinegars, oils and other condiments, and find that I use it more than I expect. I sprinkled a little rose sugar on a dish of spiced roasted skate and found the result delicate and subtle. If you are making a classic Moroccan *bistilla* for a special occasion, serve it with a sprinkling of rose sugar for an exotic and delicious touch. Otherwise, flower sugars are excellent in baking, ice-creams and custards.

Rose petal sugar

Spread the rose petals in a single layer on a clean tea-towel or kitchen paper and leave to dry for 12 hours. Put them in a food-processor with the sugar, using one part rose petals to two or three parts sugar, and process until the mixture is well blended. Unless you want the sugar for immediate use, it is important that the flowers be *completely* dry before you grind them, otherwise your food-processor will be a mass of sugar paste before you know what has happened.

heavily scented rose petals, red or deep pink
granulated sugar

Lavender sugar

To make this, take fresh lavender flower heads, allow them to dry out for an hour or two and then grind with preserving or granulated sugar. Ten parts sugar to one part flowers is usually about right, but this needs to be tested, as the concentration of fragrant oils varies from year to year, depending on the amount of sun. I usually add a couple of whole sprigs of lavender to

Lavender sugar / continued

the jar. If you prefer to keep the sugar pristine and unmixed, simply layer sugar in a large jar with lavender heads, although over time some buds will detach themselves from the stalk.

Store the sugar in an airtight container in a dark, dry place. This is best used within a year. If you keep it much longer, the lavender flavour changes from floral and subtle to something spicy, almost akin to ginger. I have found this particularly noticeable when making shortbread with year-old rather than freshly ground lavender sugar.

When making lavender sugar, you need to choose lavender in full bloom and to pick off each individual flower if you want to achieve a pure colour. If you simply separate from the stalk the flowers enclosed in the sepals, you will get a greenish sugar. The same happens with syrup.

Flower syrups

Sugar preserves the flavour and colour of sweetly scented flowers. The amount of sugar you need depends on how you plan to use the syrup. To make a poaching syrup, you will use two parts water to one part sugar. For a medium-weight syrup, of the kind you would use to soak a rum baba, for example, equal volumes of water and sugar are required. For a preserving syrup, use one and a half to two parts sugar to one part water.

This last syrup is really the most useful, as you can dilute it to make a poaching syrup. A heavy or strong syrup, it is ideal for spooning over ice-cream, or a steamed pudding in winter, for diluting with mineral water to make a refreshing drink and for using in cocktails as the sweet element – see pp.210–213 for cocktail ideas.

A more flowery flavour can be obtained by repeating the maceration process. That is, once you have soaked the petals overnight, strain the liquid into a saucepan, bring it to the boil and pour it over a fresh batch of petals. Roses, violets, jasmine and carnations can be prepared this way. For lavender, one maceration is sufficient and you only need 8 flower heads for the volume of sugar and water below.

I have experimented by infusing the petals in the boiling syrup, but, particularly with the heavy syrup, the mixture is too dense to penetrate the flowers and there is no release of colour. On the other hand, boiling water poured over even a small quantity of lavender flowers will release a wonderful clear blue colour. With roses it can be a little disconcerting to see that the water might turn a pale yellowy-green as the petals are infusing, but when you add the sugar the syrup turns a lovely and quite deep natural pink.

Carnation syrup

This easily made syrup can be used to flavour all manner of creams, custards, ice-creams and sorbets.

Boil the water, pour it over the flower petals and leave overnight. Then put all the ingredients in a saucepan and heat gently until the sugar has dissolved. Bring to the boil, simmer for 2 or 3 minutes before removing from the heat and leave until cold. Strain, bottle and label.

makes 600 ml / 20 fl oz

400 ml / 14 fl oz water
50 g / 2 oz clove pink or
    carnation petals
400 g / 14 oz granulated sugar

Elderflower syrup

I use the same method as above, but instead of measuring out the flower petals I use about 8 heads of fully open flowers and add the juice of a lemon when I add the sugar.

Rose petal syrup

This easily made syrup forms the base for rose-flavoured creams, custards, ice-creams and sorbets. Store it in the fridge or, if you wish to keep it longer, sterilise it following the method on p.59.

Boil the water, pour it over the flower petals in a bowl and leave for about three hours. You will notice that the colour fades, but the addition of sugar will restore its healthy pink blush. Put all the ingredients in a saucepan, heat gently until the sugar has dissolved, then remove from the heat and leave until cold. Strain, bottle and label.

makes 600 ml/20 fl oz

400 ml/14 fl oz water
50 g/2 oz heavily scented rose
   petals, preferably red or
   deep pink
400 g/14 oz granulated sugar

Violet or pansy syrup

Use this with fruit salads, crêpes filled with whipped cream or mascarpone, ice-creams and other desserts. If using pansies, choose only the purple ones. The infusion of violets will be closer to blue than purple. Six handfuls of flowers will weigh approximately 75 g/ 3 oz. You will need a *bain-marie* or a saucepan set over another pan of simmering water, as with these flowers the colour is more stable if the syrup does not boil.

Remove all the green parts from the flowers, put them in a non-reactive saucepan or top half of a *bain-marie* and pour on the boiling water. Remove from the heat and infuse overnight. Next day, stir in the sugar and heat the water in the *bain-marie* until the sugar has dissolved. Strain, bottle and label. This is best stored in the refrigerator, unless you want to sterilise it. In my experience, some of the flavour is lost that way, but the mixture does remain stable for longer. See p.59 for instructions on sterilising.

makes about 450 ml/½ pint

6 handfuls of flowers
300 ml/½ pint boiling water
600 g/20 oz granulated sugar

Flower vinegars

Flavoured vinegars have long been part of the cook's repertoire, especially in the countryside with easy access to a wealth of herbs and wild flowers. Flower vinegars are excellent as a dressing for delicate salad leaves, and also warm salads of fish or chicken. You can also use them in mayonnaise and hollandaise – see pp.72–3. If you are making fruit chutneys, consider using a flower vinegar, perhaps rose vinegar for a fig chutney, elderflower vinegar in a gooseberry chutney and lavender vinegar in an apple chutney. Sweet cucumber pickles are very good done in an elderflower vinegar, as are pickled herrings or salmon.

I generally use white wine vinegar, especially when making lavender vinegar (see p.34) as I like to see the contents of the bottle, but elderflowers are very good in cider vinegar, and there is no reason not to use red wine vinegar if you wish to make to make a fragrant red rose vinegar. There is now a fabulous moscatel wine vinegar made in Spain, which is the perfect vehicle for more delicate flower vinegars, especially elderflower, carnation and rose. Flowers from myrtle and fennel can also be used.

Elderflower vinegar

This subtly flavoured vinegar makes a very good dressing for salad leaves, and also goes well with warm fish or chicken salads.

Soak the labels off the bottles without opening them, then shake the flowers to remove any insects or loose pollen. Break up the elderflower heads into small sprigs and push the flowers into the vinegar bottles, first removing a little of the vinegar. Screw the tops back on and stand the bottles on a sunny window sill.

After a week or so, strain the vinegar and replace the flowers with fresh ones. Re-cork and label. If you still

makes 4 bottles

4 bottles white wine vinegar
8–12 elderflower heads

Elderflower vinegar / continued

have any of the vinegar left the following year, remove the old flowers and add some new ones. The result will be an exquisite, intensely flavoured vinegar.

Herb-flavoured vinegars can be made in exactly the same way; tarragon, sage (especially purple sage) and lemon grass all make excellent flavourings for vinegar.

Lavender vinegar

It is worth making several bottles of this vinegar during the summer. Not only does it make an excellent present, but it also retains its flavour and fragrance in a very pure form. I have one bottle which might almost be described as a mini-solera system; each year I replace the lavender flowers and top up with white wine vinegar.

Open up each bottle of vinegar and place 5 sprigs in each. Re-stopper the bottles and leave in a sunny place for 2 weeks. If you can, then replace the lavender with fresh sprigs, put the bottles back in the sunny spot and leave for a further 2 weeks. If you only have one chance to pick and use lavender, leave for three to four weeks in the sun before using the vinegar. Soak off the labels and re-label in a suitable fashion.

makes 4 bottles

4 bottles white wine vinegar
20 sprigs freshly picked lavender

Violet vinegar

Violets are so subtly scented that you need the palest, mildest vinegar you can find. I like to use coconut vinegar, which you will find where Filipino foods are sold, or a mild Japanese rice vinegar. Some supermarket white wine vinegars will also serve, as they can be very bland. Cider vinegar, however, is too dark and has too distinctive in flavour.

4 or 5 handfuls of violet flowers
1 bottle mild vinegar

Put the flowers only, with all the green parts removed, into a glass jug and pour on the vinegar. Seal the top of the jug with cling film and leave for a week or so in a sunny place for the scent and colour to transfer to the vinegar. Strain and bottle, cork and label. Keep in a dark place.

Flower vodkas

The perfume maker uses *enfleurage*, in oil or volatile solvents such as alcohol to extract the perfume from flowers. The cook can do the same. I prefer to make a single flavour, using jasmine, rose petals, violets or elderflower. Fill a bottle of vodka with freshly picked flowers, seal it and leave on a sunny window for a few days. Strain through a cloth into a jug. Fill the bottle with fresh flowers then pour in the strained vodka. Leave for a few days, then strain. For a stronger extraction, you can repeat the operation once or twice.

This method has the disadvantage of requiring many flowers over a period of two weeks or so. A less intense extraction can be made by filling a decanter with flower petals, pouring on a bottle of vodka, sealing the top with cling film and leaving to macerate in the sunniest spot for 3 or 4 weeks, by which time the flowers will have yielded their flavour and possibly some colour to the vodka. Strain into a clean bottle, label and cork.

You can add sugar syrup or leave the spirit unsweetened, if you think you might use it with savoury dishes. For example, use it to deglaze the pan after you have sautéed scallops, prawns or a chicken breast, for a subtle base for your sauce. To sweeten the mixture to make a flower liqueur, add an equal quantity of preserving syrup – see p.30.

If you wish to make lavender vodka, use only about 8 sprigs per 75 centilitre bottle, otherwise the scent and flavour will be too strong.

Flowers for decoration

Some flowers have little scent for extracting, but make attractive garnishes for salads and other dishes, as, of course, do some of the scented flowers I have written about in subsequent chapters. Among the flowers you can use for decoration are Busy Lizzies, pansies, violas, primroses, nasturtiums, cornflowers, marigold petals, hollyhocks, borage, chive flowers or those from other herbs. Nasturtiums, marigolds, chives, alliums and other herb flowers go well in savoury dishes. Marigold petals, for example, look very good against the pale creamy green of a chilled vichyssoise or lettuce soup.

The next five techniques are less about the flavour of flowers and more about their appearance and how to use them other than simply strewing them over salads. They are so pretty and effective that I think they are worth including.

Crystallised flowers

Roses, violets and mimosa are the most commonly available crystallised flowers, but it is worth knowing how to do the job yourself. It is not difficult and does not require a large number of ingredients or complicated equipment – all you need is a fine-tipped artist's paintbrush, a small fine sieve, a wire rack and baking parchment; a pair of fine tweezers can also be very useful. It is, however, delicate work, requiring patience and a little manual dexterity.

Any of the flowers mentioned in this book can be crystallised, but at first it is best to work with small, simple items, such violets, rose petals or borage flowers.

There are two ways of crystallising flowers, one using egg white, the other using gum tragacanth (see p.41). The quantities given for both methods are sufficient for about 40 small flowers or rose petals, although it is not a good idea to pick so many at once, as you run the risk of them wilting – it is far better to work with a few at a time.

Method 1

Whisk the egg white to a light foam, adding the spirit at the end. This helps the egg white and sugar to dry and therefore set more quickly. Hold the flower or petal at the base and paint it all over with the egg white, taking care to include all edges and folds between the petals. Use the sieve or your fingers gently to sprinkle on the sugar, making sure that the flower is well coated but not clogged with sugar. Place the flower on the wire rack which you have first covered with baking parchment. When you have crystallised all the flowers, put them in a cool, well-ventilated place to dry completely, when they will feel stiff and be very brittle. Carefully store them in airtight boxes lined with baking parchment, and layered between the parchment.

1 egg white
1/2 teaspoon grappa or vodka
100 g / 3 1/2 oz caster sugar

Method 2

Mix the gum tragacanth and water, then paint it on the flower and proceed as described above.

1 tablespoon gum tragacanth
3 tablespoons water
100 g / 3 1/2 oz caster sugar

Flower confetti

Flower confetti is exactly what it says. Indeed, you can throw it over a bridal couple as well as over a platter of roast chicken. To make it, you need flower petals of roughly the same size, or petals that can be rolled and shredded with a sharp knife.

They are best used within an hour or so of being gathered, laying the petals on a damp tea towel until required. Or you can dry and store them, but they will lose some of their colour. However, dried confetti is effective in a stuffing for quails or chicken, and also for scattering on smooth vegetable soups.

Bergamot, borage, chrysanthemum, cornflower, daisy and marigold petals make a splendid confetti, but throughout the book you will come across other flowers that will also lend themselves to this treatment.

Flower fritters and tempura

Deep-fried sage leaves have long been a favourite garnish, and even a cocktail snack. You can do the same thing with edible flowers, using either a fritter batter or the crisper, lighter tempura batter, which, in my view is preferable. Suitable flowers include nasturtiums, squash blossoms, day lilies, marigold fans, rose buds, sage flowers, mimosa and elderflowers.

Fritter batter

Beat all the ingredients together in bowl for a smooth, lump-free batter. When your frying oil has almost reached the correct temperature, 188°C/370°F, dip your chosen flower in the batter and allow any drips to fall back into the bowl. Drop the flower into the oil and remove after a minute or so, when the fritter will be a pale gold. Drain on paper towels and serve dusted with icing sugar.

125 g/generous 4 oz plain flour
a pinch of salt
1 large egg
300 ml/10 fl oz semi-skimmed milk
groundnut, sunflower or rapeseed oil for deep-frying
icing sugar for serving

Tempura batter

Iced water, rice flour and quick mixing are the ingredients for tempura batter. It does not matter if there are small lumps of flour in the batter, which – above all – should not be over-mixed or it will become heavy.

Whisk the egg whites and water together, then quickly whisk in the flour.

Dip in the flowers and proceed as above.

250 ml/generous 8 fl oz iced water
2 egg whites
150 g/5 oz rice flour

Flower ice bowl

I believe that Myrtle Allen of Ballymaloe, Ireland's most famous chef, was the inventor of the amazing flower ice bowl. You need two bowls of the same shape, one smaller than the other, which sits inside the larger bowl. It is vital that the larger bowl can fit in your freezer.

Pour some water into the space between the two bowls, stir in a handful of fresh flower petals or small flowers and place something reasonably heavy in the smaller bowl so that its rim is level with that of the larger bowl. Then secure the two bowls at intervals with sticky tape to ensure that the small bowl is firmly anchored in the centre and place in the freezer until solid. Add more water and flowers and freeze again, then repeat the process. The ice bowl has to be made in stages, otherwise all the flowers stay on the surface, when the effect one wants to achieve is flowers suspended in the ice.

This is perfect for serving scoops of home-made ice-cream and sorbets: a 'rose bowl', for example, filled with rose petal kulfi – see p.176.

You can also freeze individual flowers or petals in ice cubes to add to drinks.

Flower-printed pasta

I developed this recipe, which reminds me of pressing flowers as a child, from the herb-printed pasta that became popular in restaurants a few years ago. It is not difficult to do, and if you do not want to make your own pasta you can use wonton wrappers, which can be bought in Chinese shops. Use small flowers such as heartsease, violets, jasmine, rosemary flowers, sage flowers, or petals from roses, marigolds or cornflowers.

makes 24 sheets

48 squares of thinly rolled home-made pasta or wonton wrappers
1 tablespoon cornflour
3 tablespoons water
flowers

You can serve two sheets of the pasta as a large open raviolo, without sealing the edges, and put a spoonful of luxurious filling between the sheets – crab meat, cooked and chopped wild and cultivated mushrooms, shredded goose or duck mixed with ginger, soy and spring onions all make delicious fillings.

Keep the pasta covered with a damp cloth and use two pieces at a time. Mix the water and cornflour and brush one surface of each wrapper with the 'paste'. Arrange the flowers on one of them. Press the other piece on top and cut decorative, fluted edges with a pasta cutter. Place on a clean tea-towel and continue with the remaining wrappers. Cook in a large, shallow pan of boiling water, then remove with a slotted spoon, drain and fold in oil before serving hot or cold.

You can fold the squares diagonally to make triangular pasta. You can also make flower-printed lasagna very easily with a hand-cranked pasta roller. Having rolled out two sheets of pasta to the third notch, arrange the flowers on one sheet and cover with the other, pressing down firmly. Put the rollers back to the widest setting and roll the pasta through, then on each progressively narrower setting. You will see that the flowers stretch too, and that you may not be able to roll it through the last setting without tearing the pasta.

Other ingredients for cooking with flowers

Sugar

I normally use organic golden granulated or caster sugar in my cooking, as it is slightly less refined than white sugar. In my flower desserts, however, I always use refined sugar as I want nothing to detract from the pure colour of the flower extracted in the syrup, cream, cordial or jelly.

The best sugar for making jams and jellies is that with the largest crystals, as this dissolves slowly, minimising scum and producing a nice clarity in the finished product. If it is available, use preserving sugar, which has extra large crystals. Cooks in the US and other countries where preserving sugar is not available can use granulated sugar, which is an excellent all-round sugar, whatever preserves you are making. Jam sugar, which contains pectin and citric acid, is a great boon when making jams and jellies from ingredients such as flower infusions, strawberries and figs which lack or are low in pectin, as the preserve always sets when you follow the directions on the packet. Where jam sugar is not available and the recipe does not call for an extract of cooked apples, use liquid or powdered pectin, following the instructions on the label.

Gum tragacanth

Also known as powdered tragacanth or gum Arabic, this is used for preserving and frosting flower petals. It is no longer widely available, and is now most easily bought on order through independent high street pharmacies. If you can buy it, mix 1 teaspoon of the powder with 1 tablespoon of water and brush it on the petals before dipping in caster or icing sugar. The alternative is to use whisked egg white, as described on p.37.

Apples

These are invaluable when making flower jellies, and
I have often used other than cooking apples. Granny
Smiths are ideal, as they are tart but do not burst.
Bramleys can be a problem, because they cook to such
a soft mass that some of this escapes into the extracted
liquid used when making jellies, although they are
fine in jams and chutneys. One of the most unusual
cooking apples I have used is the White Transparent,
a Russian variety, which produces a very pale extract,
and therefore a pale jelly; this is particularly useful
when using pale flowers such as pink roses or
carnations, elderflower or jasmine.

Equipment for cooking with flowers

Tea filters, which look like large, open tea bags, are
ideal for infusing fresh flowers and petals. These are
quite long and large and allow plenty of room, even
for larger flowers and buds. Disposing of them when
used is very simple.

The grinder attachment on a stick blender is perfect
for grinding dry flower sugars. Alternatively, you can
keep a separate coffee-grinder and use it only for
flowers and spices, provided you brush it out well after
using it so that flavours do not taint the next batch of
ingredients.

For small quantities of flower pastes and conserves,
where fresh – and therefore moist – flowers are used,
there is nothing better than the traditional English
stoneware pestle and mortar. It was the ideal
implement for pounding and grinding fresh herbs and
flowers in Elizabethan days, and it still is.

To store these scented delicacies, plastic boxes with
airtight lids keep all the flower scent in and other
fridge smells out. They are especially useful if you are
making flavoured butter or want to store a flower
cream or custard.

I save any elegant empty bottles – grappa bottles are especially handsome – as these make excellent containers for flower vinegars and cordials given as presents.

There are some items of equipment I highly recommend to help with your baking and dessert-making, and a browse through a good kitchenware shop or mail order catalogue will provide further inspiration. Professionals use Silpat baking sheets, which are available from catering suppliers, but you can find similar non-stick products for domestic cooks. The cook's blow-torch is a delight to use, easy to operate and, with a neat, precise flame, ideal for caramelising crème brulée.

Wire racks for cooling cakes and pastries are essential, and you can now buy multi-tiered racks, which are particularly useful if you are baking in quantity.

If you intend to crystallise flowers, it is worth investing in a couple of fine water colour paint brushes for applying the egg white and a small sieve for sifting on the sugar. A fine-gauge rack for drying the flowers or petals after crystallising is also a good idea, as is a roll of good quality wax paper for storing crystallised flowers in layers in airtight boxes

A fine-gauge spray bottle is useful if you want no more than a mist of flower water over a dessert or fruit salad. Consider too, if you are serving a dessert buffet, that you might just want to perfume the air around it with rose water.

Shopping for flower flavours

Whenever I go to Toulouse I try to visit a good *épicerie* and stock up on *violettes de Toulouse*, crystallised flowers, not the violet-flavoured sweets. These are very good, as are the *guimauves à la violette*, violet-flavoured marshmallows. Last time I was there I also bought *sirop de violette*, knowing that I would never find myself with enough fresh violets to make a bottle of violet syrup. The flavour was subtle, but the colour seemed to have been ruined by an overdose of blue food colouring. The first time I made violet ice-cream the result was an unappetising blue. Subsequently I tempered the mixture with red food colouring, and that produced, in my view, the right shade. Reading Hannah Glasse and other eighteenth-century authors, however, it would appear that one of the uses of violet syrup was in fact to colour desserts blue.

Nevertheless, I love the scented flavour of violets, and was thrilled to find an array of culinary essences in Les Grandes Epiceries de Paris, in rue de Sèvres, perhaps the best food shop in Paris. Made by Chabaud C&S in Montpellier, the essences come in a wide range of herb, spice and flower extracts. Amongst the cinnamon, basil and lemon grass, I found rose, violet and jasmine. These come in 15 ml bottles with a dropper and are very expensive, but a little goes a long way and I consider them an excellent investment.

Much less costly are the floral waters, especially orange flower water, rosewater and occasionally lavender water. These are the by-products from the distillation of essential oils. There are some English manufacturers of rosewater and orange flower water, but far and away the best I have found are those from the Lebanon, especially the Cortas brand, which are sold in Middle Eastern food shops and some of the better food halls. The Hop Shop in Kent, which can be contacted on www.hopshop.co.uk, produces very fine culinary lavender essences from home-grown English lavender, one for baking and hot dishes and one for creams and ices.

You will find rose essence, or rose oil, of which you only need a drop or two, in Indian shops, and also rose petal powder, made from dried and ground rose petals. This is an excellent ingredient, which I have used in sponge cakes and rose petal kulfi.
An American range of natural essences and flower waters under the Star Kay White label is available in the baking or specialist sections of some supermarkets,

as well as from Lakeland by mail order. Their rose essence is fine, and a little goes a long way.

Turkish rose petal jam, *gül receli*, is quite delicious and I try to keep a jar on hand, especially in the spring and early summer when my own rose syrups, sugars and jellies tend to have run out.

The Oxfordshire-based company Fidde & Payne produce small jars of natural crystallised rose petals and violets that may be found in the baking sections of good supermarkets and foods shops, as well as in shops specialising in cake decoration.

Other floral ingredients are widely available in health food stores and at the tea counter, especially dried camomile and linden (lime) flowers, both of which have uses other than making tisanes. You will find rose, chrysanthemum and jasmine teas – all of them quite fragrant with those flowers – in Chinese food shops.

There are flower jellies and preserves available, some better than others. It puzzles me that anyone would think it a good idea to combine lavender and violet in a jelly, however, as each flavour cancels out the other. Much better to make your own.

Flower liqueurs used to be very popular in the 1800s, especially the Italian Rosolio. Versions of Rosolio di Rosa are still made today, especially in Sicily, and are worth tracking down when on your travels. Combier, a 150-year-old distillery in Saumur, has revived the art of making flower liqueurs and recently launched a Liqueur de Violette and a Liqueur de Rose, both of which have very pure, intense and natural flavours and aromas.

Flowers and fruit

There are flower and fruit combinations that, in my experience, work particularly well. With this and the basic recipes scattered throughout the book you can develop your own recipes using these combinations or others that you find to your liking.

Elderflower – gooseberries, strawberries, cherries, white peaches and nectarines, loquats, honeydew melon, green Muscat grapes, green figs.

Hibiscus – cranberries, redcurrants, bananas, pineapple.

Jasmine – mango, guava, lychees, pineapple, strawberries.

Lavender – apricot, canteloupe and charentais melons, peaches, blackcurrants, lemons, purple figs.

Orange flower – oranges, citrus fruit, strawberries, pineapple, green figs.

Rose – strawberries, raspberries, cherries, lychees, guavas, custard apple, melons, oranges, purple figs.

Saffron – Seville (bitter) orange, peach, apricot, mango.

Violet – blackcurrants, purple figs, black Muscat grapes, honeydew melons.

Some practical advice on cooking with flowers

Do not eat anything that you cannot identify simply because it smells as though it would taste good.

Even if you know a flower to be edible, such as a rose, do not use it for culinary purposes if you think it may have been sprayed with harmful substances such as pesticides. **Flowers purchased from high-street florists or supermarkets should not be used in the kitchen**, as these will almost certainly have undergone spraying and other chemical treatment. You should only eat bought flowers if they come from a florist who can guarantee that they have not been sprayed.

Flowers growing on grass verges may have been exposed to carbon monoxide fumes, animal excrement and other waste, so, however attractive they may seem, they are best left where they are.

It is not advisable to use flowers in the kitchen if you suffer from asthma, hay-fever or other allergies. This includes skin allergies, as handling certain flowers may exacerbate the condition. Some flowers, such as lavender and fennel, have powerful therapeutic properties, and should not be taken in large quantities, especially when pregnant.

Many of the flowers traditionally used in cooking, such as violets, primroses, mallow and cowslips, are wild flowers. The countryside is no longer carpeted with wild flower meadows – those that remain are part of our dwindling natural heritage and should be preserved.

There are certain protected species of wild flowers that cannot be picked. Some people feel that we should not pick any wild flowers, while others believe that, where there is an abundance, a light picking will not cause any harm. Wild flowers should never be uprooted for transplanting to your own garden. It may be illegal to do so; it is certainly anti-social.

Fortunately, specialist seed merchants can supply wild flower seeds, so there is no reason why you should not grow your own if you want to make violet syrup or cowslip wine.

It is best to pick flowers on a dry day, and in the early part of the day, after the dew has dried but before the sun is hot enough to evaporate the essential oils. Choose fully open specimens, undamaged by insects or disease. Shake them to remove any tiny insects. Use your judgement as to whether or not the flowers should be rinsed. If so, do it quickly in ice cold water, and lay the flowers to dry on two or three layers of paper towels before proceeding with the recipe. It is best to use the flowers within a few hours of picking,

but if you do need to store them for a day or two,
surround them with a damp – not wet – tea-towel
and seal them in an airtight box in the refrigerator.

To dry flower petals

Place the petals in a single layer on a foil-lined baking
sheet and put this in the oven set at 100°C/200°F/
gas mark $\frac{1}{4}$ for about 2 hours or until the petals are
dry enough to crumble. Store them in an airtight jar
in a cool, dark place and use them as you would other
herbs, within 12 months, until the flowers are in
bloom again.

Flower identification

In cases where the flower's common name identifies it
unambiguously, I have used that common name –
rose, lavender etc. Where a number of flowers go by
similar names, I have used the Latin name to further
identify the flower I am referring to. Jasmine on p.151
is a good example.

Protected species

English Nature (www.english-nature.org.uk)
and the Joint Nature Conservation Committee
(www.jncc.org.uk) are among the best sources of
guidance, highlighting the different pieces of
legislation that protect certain flowers, and also the
European Directives dealing with the same subject.

Carnations and gilly flowers

Seventeenth- and eighteenth-century English households used considerable quantities of clove gilly flowers for salads, soups and desserts, candying the flowers for decoration of cakes, fools and custards, and also as a soothing cordial for coughs and sore throats.

So much more attractive a name than 'carnation', the gilly – or July – flower denotes the family of sweetly scented flowers that include clove pinks, phlox, Sweet Williams and the stiffly formal carnation. To a greater or lesser degree, the spicy smell of cloves enveloped in a cloud of their sweet fragrance is the distinguishing feature of the entire family. Choose the most perfumed flowers you can from amongst the pinks and carnations.

Carnations have always been one of my favourite flowers and were amongst the first that I cooked in public when I presented a promotion of English food at London's Intercontinental Hotel in 1987. As well as lavender sorbet, we made a carnation ice-cream, somewhat to the consternation of the brilliant, although rather conservative, Swiss pastry chef, Ernst Bachmann, but to the delight of the customers.

Sourcing large quantities of fragrant, unsprayed carnations was not the least of our problems and, because of the amounts involved, we definitely did not remove the 'white part'. Chef Bachmann and I

'Carnation gillyflowers for beauty and delicate smell and excellent properties, deserve letters of gold'

Stephen Blake, *The Complete Gardener's Practice*, 1664

did a test and found that neither the colour nor the flavour of the syrup was impaired in any way. I vividly remember standing over a large stockpot of simmering syrup and flower petals, stirring from time to time while watched by a couple of bewildered commis chefs – I felt like a white witch. Then we strained the syrup, cooled it and mixed it with a creamy custard. The result was a lilac-pink ice-cream, sweet and subtly spicy at the same time, perfect with a finger or two of shortbread. It was written about in more than one restaurant column, as was the lavender sorbet, and I confess to feeling rather flattered when Derek Cooper referred to it in a speech making fun of food fashions.

Carnation wine cordial

Sops-in-wine were carnation petals floated on the celebratory wine served to a betrothed couple in sixteenth-century England, and was also the name of a variety of small clove pink. This is an up-to-date version, which produces something resembling a vermouth. Enjoy it as a long drink with a slice of orange and sparkling mineral water. Splash it on a summer salad of strawberries and raspberries or use it in a sauce to accompany summer pudding. A full-bodied Sicilian wine makes a perfect base for this cordial.

Put all the ingredients except for the brandy in a saucepan, bring to the boil, simmer for 5 minutes, remove from the heat and leave overnight. Strain the liquid, stir in the brandy, then bottle, seal and label.

makes one 75 cl bottle

one 75 cl bottle red wine
2 handfuls clove pink or
  carnation flowers
200–250 g/7–8 oz
  granulated sugar
3 cloves
seeds of 2 cardamom pods
a generous curl of thinly pared
  orange zest
4 tablespoons brandy

White carnation mousse

A white chocolate mousse has a slightly creamier texture than one made with dark chocolate, so I use a little gelatine to give a firmer set. As always, it pays to buy a good quality chocolate.

Break up the chocolate and melt it in a bowl set over hot water. Sprinkle the gelatine over a couple of tablespoons of water in a small Pyrex jug or similar, until soft. When the chocolate has melted, remove the bowl from the hot water and allow the chocolate to cool slightly. Stand the jug with gelatine in hot water until the gelatine has completely dissolved, then add the syrup and stir into the melted chocolate. Add the cream gradually, beating to keep it smooth.

If you put very cold cream into very hot chocolate, the chocolate will seize up and become hard, so make sure that both are at similar tepid temperatures when you combine them. Whisk the egg whites and gradually mix them into the scented chocolate. Spoon into ramekins or simply into a container that can be stored in the refrigerator.

To serve, scoop out quenelles and shape them with two dessertspoons. Decorate with carnation petals before serving. This mousse also makes an excellent filling for sponge cakes.

This recipe uses raw egg

serves 6

150 g / 5 oz white chocolate
1 teaspoon powdered gelatine
2 tablespoons carnation syrup
    (p.31)
1 tablespoon clove carnation
    petals, blanched and shredded
150 ml / 5 fl oz double cream,
    at room temperature
2 egg whites

Pear and carnation soufflés with carnation wine sauce

Cook the pears in the water and sugar until soft, which will take 10 to 15 minutes if they are ripe, up to 40 minutes if hard. Generously butter individual soufflé dishes and dust their insides with caster sugar. Refrigerate until needed. Put the fruit in a sieve over a bowl and let the syrup drip through. Retain the syrup and then transfer the pears to a bowl and mash them to a smooth purée.

Melt the butter in a saucepan and stir in the flour. Cook the roux for a few minutes and then blend in equal parts of pear syrup and skimmed milk, no more than 300 ml/$\frac{1}{2}$ pint in all, until you have a smooth sauce. Cook for a few minutes until it thickens.

Remove from the heat and stir in the pear purée, the flower petals and the egg yolks. Mix thoroughly.

Whisk the egg whites to firm peaks and gently fold into the pear mixture. Spoon the mixture into the prepared soufflé dishes and place them in a roasting tin containing enough water to come one-third of the way up the sides of the dishes.

Bake for 12 to 15 minutes in an oven pre-heated to 200°C / 400°F / gas mark 6. Meanwhile, make the sauce by blending the cordial and cornflour, bringing it to the boil and cooking for a few minutes until it has thickened slightly.

Dust the soufflés with icing sugar and, as you serve each one, break open the top with a spoon and pour in a little sauce, which will cause the soufflé to rise in its dish.

Cook's tip

If you prefer a creamy sauce, omit the cornflour and instead add 150 ml/5 fl oz of double cream to the sauce, letting it boil until slightly thickened.

serves 4 to 6

Soufflés
500 g / 1 lb peeled, cored and
    quartered pears
2 tablespoons water
100 g / 4 oz granulated sugar
25 g / 1 oz butter, softened
2 tablespoons plain flour
150 ml / 5 fl oz skimmed milk
1 tablespoon caster sugar
a handful of clove pink or
    carnation petals, shredded
3 eggs, separated
icing sugar for dusting

Sauce
150 ml / 5 fl oz carnation wine
    cordial (p.50)
1 teaspoon cornflour

Spice-cured salmon

Curing salmon with salt is one of the best methods I know of preparing fish for the table. Over the years I have strayed wildly from the original recipe, the famous Scandinavian gravlax that uses dill as a flavouring, and have cured salmon in a peaty Islay malt with fresh thyme, in green tea leaves and soy sauce, and also with flowers. Try this variation, using wild rather than farmed salmon if you can find it.

Scale and fillet the fish, removing as many bones as possible. Make the seasoning by mixing together the salt, sugar, pepper and cloves.

Spread a third of the petals in the bottom of a rectangular dish large enough to take the piece of fish. Spoon 3 tablespoons of seasoning over the petals and lay 1 salmon fillet on top, skin side down. Spread the rest of the mixture on the flesh side of both salmon fillets and sandwich them together with two-thirds of the remaining flower petals laid between them.

The rest of the seasoning should be spread on the skin side of the top fillet, covered with the remaining flower petals, the whole thing covered with food wrap and weighted down for 2 to 3 days. Refrigerate the salmon during this time.

To serve, scrape off the petals and salt, drain off the liquid and slice thinly across the grain, or in thicker slices vertically down to the skin.

Serve with a sweet, spiced mayonnaise and a few carnation petals for garnish. Use a dash of carnation syrup and vinegar if you have it; if not, honey, a pinch of ground cloves and lime juice or cider vinegar added to a home-made mayonnaise will be almost as good.

serves 8

1 salmon tail, weighing about
   1.5 kg/generous 3 lb
5 tablespoons coarse sea salt
2 tablespoons light muscovado
   sugar
2 tablespoons freshly ground
   black pepper
1 teaspoon ground cloves
2 or 3 handfuls of clove pink or
   carnation petals

Braised lamb shanks with summer vegetables and carnation sauce

Here lamb is served with carnation sauce in which the flowers are steeped in a mild vinegar, rather like a mint sauce. It is very delicate, and makes an excellent partner for new season's lamb and young vegetables.

First make the sauce by grinding the petals in a mortar with the sugar and salt, then working in the honey and vinegar. Add the cloves and leave to steep while you cook the lamb and vegetables.

Fry the onion in the oil in a casserole until golden brown, then add the garlic. Brown the lamb shanks all over, and then nail a bay leaf to each piece of meat, securing it with two cloves. Add the wine and peppercorns, bring to the boil, cover and simmer for 1 hour.

Meanwhile, prepare the vegetables – baby leeks, courgettes, new carrots, small onions, green beans, a selection of what you like, but all cut to roughly the same thickness to ensure even cooking. Add the vegetables after the lamb has cooked for an hour, stir to cover them with juice and then continue cooking until the lamb and vegetables are tender.

The casserole can also be cooked in the oven at 180°C / 350°F / gas mark 4 for about 2 hours, or for longer at a lower temperature if this is more convenient.

Check the flavour of the carnation sauce, as it may require a little more vinegar or sugar.

serves 4

Sauce

2 tablespoons carnation petals
1 tablespoon granulated sugar
a pinch of sea salt
1 tablespoon honey
2 or 3 tablespoons cider or
   coconut vinegar
2 cloves

Lamb shanks

1 large onion, sliced or chopped
1 tablespoon olive or sunflower oil
2–3 garlic cloves, crushed
8 cloves
4 bay leaves
4 lamb shanks
300 ml / ½ pint red or white wine,
   lamb stock or water
1 teaspoon black peppercorns
500 g / 1 lb vegetables, prepared
   weight – see recipe
salt

Cherry-stuffed quails with carnation sauce

Sweet and sour flavours add interest to what can sometimes be a rather bland bird and help to turn this into a dish for a special occasion. This method can also be used for stuffed chicken, duck or guinea fowl breasts. I have not specified what cherries to use, as there is usually only one variety on the market at any given time – this recipe works with them all.

Lightly season the quail, which should have the breastbone or rib cage removed, inside and out with salt, pepper and a pinch of ground cloves. Fry the shallots in half the butter until translucent, then stir in the breadcrumbs, most of the carnation petals, keeping some back to use as a garnish, and a spoonful of the cordial to moisten the mixture. Chop half the cherries and add them to the stuffing. Stuff the quails and secure them closed with toothpicks.

Fry the birds all over in the remaining butter in a lidded, oven-proof pan, splash in the rest of the cordial, bring to the boil, cover and simmer for 30 minutes. Add the cherries and cook until the quail are tender, which will probably take another 10 to 15 minutes.

Wild rice goes well with the sweet and savoury quails; you will need to start cooking it before the quails. Make a heap of rice on each plate, sit the quail on top and spoon the sauce around it.

serves 2

2 quails, partially boned
salt
pepper
a pinch of ground cloves
2 shallots, chopped
25 g / 1 oz butter
50 g / 2 oz fresh breadcrumbs
a handful of fresh carnation petals
50 ml / 2 fl oz carnation wine
    cordial (p.50)
150 g / 5 oz cherries, stoned

Elderflower and hawthorn blossom

It never ceases to delight me that such lively and attractive blossoms are to be found amongst the dull leaves and rank twigs of elder trees. Every May I keep watch for the first lacy umbels on the trees on Hampstead Heath, and a few days later I am out foraging with a couple of bags and a walking stick, an essential tool because the creamier, denser panicles always seem to be higher up, turning towards the sun. I fill the bags loosely so as not to bruise the delicate blooms. Before putting them in the bag, I shake the blossoms lightly to remove the larger wild life. Smaller creepy-crawlies will, I'm afraid, have to take their chances and disappear before the syrup-boiling stage, as I never wash the blossoms, but just give them another light shake once I get them home, because I am convinced that dousing them in water removes some of their fragrance. If I have inadvertently picked any flower heads that are really infested with bugs, I of course discard them, and when I make elderflower syrup, jelly or cordial I always strain it through a cloth-lined sieve, which takes care of any tiny ants or other insect life that might still be clinging to the flowers, and also of the pollen, which makes the liquid cloudy.

On one occasion when I wrote about elderflowers in my newspaper column, a reader complained that I should have warned people to pick only certain types of elder blossom, that some is fragrant and some

'Some persons hold themselves entitled, after two or three times receiving a piece of shortbread and a glass of elderflower wine, to ask the lady who has given them such refreshment, in marriage.'

M. Lindsay

unpleasant. I have never found this to be the case –
indeed, after 25 years of cooking with elderflowers,
I would say that the blossom often has little fragrance.
It is only when it is steeped in syrup, added to
gooseberry jam or made into a jelly that the
characteristic muscatel flavour is released. For that,
above all, is the great glory of the humble elderflower
– it is transformed, not by alchemy but by a very
simple process, from hedgerow food into an elegant
and complex ingredient.

The distinctive muscatel flavour lends itself above all
to desserts and a variety of sweet preparations, but one
savoury dish I came across recently deserves a
mention. Springtime in northern Italy brings with it
carpets of wild flowers in the alpine meadows and
hedgerows. In Rovereto, east of Lake Garda, the
restaurants were celebrating spring with dishes created
from local flowers. We were served a salad on black
plates, over which were scattered hawthorn and
elderflowers, daisies and other white blossoms. It was
fragrant and beautiful, and certainly worth copying at
home. Try it with a delicate seafood salad, perhaps
prawns, scallops or white crab meat.

When I was filming a television series in the West
Country, I harvested all manner of fruit, flowers and
herbs to preserve as jams, jellies, pickles and cordials.
That summer I gathered armfuls of elderflowers and
my cordial was dispensed to friends and family, my
only regret being that I had not made even more
bottles.

For me, hawthorn blossoms do not hold the same
exciting possibilities as elderflowers. True, they make a
very pleasing addition to a wine cup, the traditional
German *Maibowle*. In the Middle Ages, when flower
pottages were common, a dish not unlike a custard
called *spinée* was served: the hawthorn flowers were
pounded, mixed with almond milk and starch, such as
wheat flour, beaten with eggs and then cooked. The
dish was garnished with hawthorn leaves and flowers
before serving. Medieval apple pottage was sometimes
served decorated with apple blossom. Both hawthorn

flowers and apple blossom are certainly very pretty, smell sweet and are most attractive when strewn on a green salad.

Dorothy Hartley has a wonderfully rustic recipe for hawthorn flower liqueur, for which you need to gather a good quantity of blossoms, although only the flower heads are used. These are packed, but not squashed, into a wide-mouthed bottle. Add 3 or 4 tablespoons of granulated sugar, top up with brandy, seal tightly and leave in a sunny place for a few days to warm the mixture and dissolve the sugar. Turn upside down a few times, then store in a warm dark place for three months without disturbing. Decant carefully into a smaller bottle and keep tightly corked. The resulting ratafia-style liqueur has a subtle almondy scent.

Elderflower syrup

Shake any pollen and insects from the flower heads and strip the blossom from the main stalks. Put the elderflowers in a saucepan, together with the finely peeled zest from the lemons. Boil the water and pour it over the blossoms. Bring back to the boil, simmer for 5 minutes, then remove from the heat and allow to infuse until cold.

makes about 2 litres / 4 pints

20–30 elderflower heads
4 lemons
1.5 litres / 2½ pints water
1.5 kg / 3 lb granulated sugar

Warm the bottles in the oven for 15 minutes at 180°C/350°F/gas mark 4. Place a sieve lined with damp muslin over a clean saucepan. Squeeze the lemons and pour their juice through the muslin before straining the infused elderflower liquid through the sieve.

Stir in the sugar, heat gently until it has dissolved and then boil for 5 minutes. Remove the pan from the heat and pour the syrup into the hot bottles. Seal, label and store the bottles in a dark place or refrigerate them. For longer keeping, the bottles of syrup can be sterilised – see p.59.

Elderflower cordial

Elderflower cordial makes a very refreshing drink when mixed with sparkling mineral water, a fine cocktail when combined with gin and sparkling water, and also an excellent flavouring for custards and ice-creams. I try to make several bottles every year, hoping that they will last until the next season.

Put the sugar and water in a saucepan, dissolve the sugar and bring to the boil. Shake the flower heads thoroughly and remove the stalks. Drop the elderflowers into the water and return to the boil. Meanwhile, put the sliced citrus fruit in a bowl or large jug with the tartaric acid, take the syrup and elderflowers off the heat and pour them over the citrus fruit. Stir well, cover loosely and leave for 24 hours before sieving and bottling. Keeps for 2 to 3 months, or longer if refrigerated.

makes about 1 litre/2 pints

1 kg/2 lb granulated sugar
1 litre/2 pints water
15 elderflower heads
2 oranges, thinly sliced
2 lemons, thinly sliced
2 limes, thinly sliced
1–2 teaspoons tartaric acid

Cook's tip

Add the smaller amount of tartaric acid, and use more only if you think it needs it. Too much tartaric acid will give the flavour of a processed commercial product. It is, of course, the tartaric acid that increases the cordial's keeping quality.

To sterilise syrups and cordials

Sterilise corks, caps or stoppers by keeping them in boiling water for 15 minutes. Fill the bottle using a funnel to 1½ inches/4 cm below the base of the cork or screw cap. Corks will need to be tied or wired down or the heat will force them out. Put the bottles in a deep saucepan and add water up to the base of the cork, heat the water to boiling point, cover the pan and maintain the water at a steady simmer for 20 minutes. Turn off the heat. Use tongs to take the bottles out of the water and stand them on a wooden tray to cool. Label and store in a cool dark place.

Elderflower sparkler

This sparkling elderflower drink is the traditional elderflower 'champagne', made in country kitchens and still-rooms for centuries. Such concoctions seem to have a mind of their own and because wild yeasts are involved they can act in unpredictable ways, such as exploding.

Put the flower heads into a large bowl. Add the sugar, the zest of the lemon finely pared, its juice and half the lemon skin, the vinegar and water – you can use either tap or bottled water, as you prefer. Cover loosely and leave for 24 to 36 hours. Strain through fine cheesecloth or muslin and bottle in screw-top or corked bottles. Leave for three weeks before serving, chilled.

Alternatively, make elderflower syrup or cordial and dilute it with sparkling mineral water.

makes about 4 litres/8 pints

10–12 large elderflower heads
500 g/1 lb granulated sugar
1 lemon
2 tablespoons white wine vinegar
4 litres/8 pints still cold water

Elderflower milk punch

A flavoured milk punch might sound as if it comes straight from the pages of a Victorian novel, but do try this – it is subtle, delicate and most refreshing when served chilled.

Strip the flowers from the stems and put them in a bowl with the honey, lemon slices and cognac and a grating of nutmeg to taste. Scald the milk, pour it over the ingredients in the bowl and leave to stand until cool. Strain into glasses and serve. It is also very good as a hot punch, but the flavours have longer to develop if the milk is allowed to cool.

serves 4–6

4 elderflower heads
1–2 tablespoons clear honey
   or sugar
half a lemon, seeded and thinly
   sliced
3–4 tablespoons cognac
nutmeg
600 ml/1 pint milk

Elderflower jelly

An inexpensive, yet delicious, early summer treat, you can't make enough of this jelly, which always makes a very welcome present.

Remove as much stalk as possible from the elderflowers and put them in a saucepan. Pour on the boiling water, bring back to the boil and simmer for 5 minutes. Then remove from the heat and allow the flowers to steep for several hours or overnight.

Put a fine muslin or lawn cloth in a sieve and ladle in the liquid and blossoms. Press down to extract as much liquid as possible and then discard the flowers. Pour the citrus juices through a sieve into a measuring jug and add the elderflower extract, bringing the liquid up to a total of 500 ml/18 fl oz. Put the liquid and sugar into a heavy saucepan, stirring in the tartaric acid. Heat gently until the sugar has dissolved, then bring to the boil and keep at a fierce boil for 4 minutes, by which time the mixture should jell. Pour into hot jars, seal, label and store in a dark place to keep the jelly nice and pale.

makes 750 g/1½ lb

10 elderflower heads
600 ml/1 pint water
juice of 1 lemon
juice of 1 lime
juice of half an orange
½ teaspoon tartaric acid .
500 g/18 oz jam sugar (that is, sugar with added pectin)

Cook's tip

If jam sugar is unavailable, use granulated sugar plus commercial pectin in liquid or powder form, and follow the manufacturer's instructions.

White peach and elderflower jam

The early white peaches usually arrive from Spain just as the first elders are coming into blossom. This jam is an extravagance unless there happens to be a glut of white peaches, even though I stretch it by using a good old Bramley, which has excellent setting qualities.

makes about 1.5 kg/3 lb

1 kg/2 lb white peaches
1 large Bramley apple
6 elderflower heads, tied in muslin
1 kg/2 lb preserving sugar

Have your clean jars heating in the oven while you prepare the fruit. Peel and core the apple, and dice very small. Halve the peaches, discarding their stones, and chop the fruit very finely. There is no need to remove the skin. Put the apple in a saucepan with 150–200 ml/5–7 fl oz of water. Cook until the fruit is soft and then add the peaches and elderflowers. Cook until these too are soft and the apple has disintegrated.

Strain the juices into a jam or other suitable pan and add the preserving sugar. Heat gently until the sugar has dissolved, boil the syrup for two minutes and then add the fruit. Stir well, bring back to the boil, skim any foam from the surface and boil until setting point is reached. This will take 3 or 4 minutes.

Remove the pan from the heat, remove the soggy parcel of elderflowers and fill hot jars with the jam. Cover with waxed paper discs and screw-top lids or cellophane covers. Label and store in a cool dark place.

Cook's tip

This jam also works very well with white nectarines. In the absence of Bramleys, any tart apple will do.

Compote of loquats with elderflowers

This is every bit as delicate and delicious as gooseberries with elderflowers, and the seasons coincide happily as the first loquats arrive from Spain and Turkey just as the elderflowers are in full bloom.

Peel the loquats, as their skin is rather tough. Halve them and twist to separate the halves. Remove and discard the large shiny brown stones and put the fruit in a saucepan, together with the syrup. Heat gently and poach for 15 minutes. Transfer the fruit to a glass bowl and strain the syrup over it. Cover and chill until required. Just before serving, decorate with a few sprigs of elderflower.

You can turn this into a delicious hot pudding by adding a crumble topping, with plenty of flaked almonds for crunch, and baking in the oven until golden brown.

serves 8

1 kg / 2 lb ripe loquats
100 ml / 4 fl oz elderflower syrup
  (p.58)
2 or 3 elderflowers heads for
  decoration

Gooseberry and elderflower crumble

The addition of a couple of sprigs of elderflowers gives an ambrosial flavour to one of the most appealing of all traditional English puddings.

Simmer the gooseberries with the elderflowers in 2-3 tablespoons of water for 10 to 15 minutes. Remove the flowers, sweeten the fruit to taste and transfer it to a buttered baking dish or individual ramekins.

Rub the butter and flour together, stir in the ground almonds and sugar, keeping the mixture loose. Spoon the crumble over the fruit and scatter on the flaked almonds. Bake for 15 minutes at 200°C/400°F/gas mark 6.

Serve either warm or hot, with cream, ice-cream or, best of all, an elderflower custard.

serves 4 to 6

For the filling
1 kg / 2 lb gooseberries, topped
  and tailed
2 large elderflower heads
golden granulated or light
  muscovado sugar to taste

For the crumble
125 g / 5 oz flour
75 g / 3 oz butter
50 g / 2 oz ground almonds
75 g / 3 oz light muscovado sugar
25 g / 1 oz flaked almonds

Elderflower custard

This delicate custard goes well with numerous baked fruit desserts in addition to gooseberry crumble. Try it with apricot tart, peach crumble or a cherry clafoutis.

Put the cream and elderflowers in a saucepan and bring gently to the boil. Mix the sugar and egg yolks in a bowl and pour on the scalded cream, including the flowers, stirring well. Pour back into the saucepan and cook very gently for a couple of minutes, stirring continuously. Take care that the custard does not boil and so curdle. Remove from the heat and leave to cool before refrigerating. This will also allow the elderflower to infuse. Cover the surface with a butter paper or cling film to prevent a skin from forming and remove the flowers before using.

serves 4 to 6

600 ml/20 fl oz single cream
2 or 3 elderflower heads, well
  shaken
125 g/4 oz golden caster sugar
8 egg yolks

Cook's tip

An alternative method is to make a standard custard, using 125 ml/4 fl oz of elderflower syrup (p.58) or cordial (p.59) in place of the sugar and adding an extra egg yolk. This has the great advantage of allowing you to make elderflower custard at any time of year. It makes the most heavenly trifle.

To make elderflower ice-cream, simply freeze the cooled custard in an ice-cream maker.

Elderflower stone ice-cream with poached gooseberries

Ice-cream beaten and mixed on a slate or marble slab has become very fashionable in North America, and it is easy to do at home if you have a marble pastry slab in your kitchen. You also need a couple of heavy paddles, but I find a couple of cleavers work quite well.

Rinse the gooseberries (there is no need to top and tail them as they will be sieved) and then poach them in 3 tablespoons of the cordial until tender. Sieve, cool and refrigerate until required. You can do this the day before preparing the ice-cream.

Remove the ice-cream from the freezer 10 minutes or so before you want to work it. Spoon it onto a clean marble or slate work-top and beat and shovel it with your utensils, working in 2 or 3 tablespoons of elderflower cordial, or more if it looks as if it will take it. Crush the meringues into large chunks, fold them into the ice-cream and serve in bowls with the gooseberry sauce.

serves 8

500 g/1 lb gooseberries, topped and tailed
150 ml/5 fl oz elderflower cordial (p.59)
1 litre/2 pints vanilla ice-cream
6 meringues

Cook's tip

Try the same method using lavender with blueberries or apricots and roses with raspberries or strawberries.

Elderflower tart

A custard recipe always leaves you with far more egg whites than you know what to do with. This recipe, based on the medieval sambocade, makes the most of them and, by using only egg whites, keeps the tart filling elegantly pale. You can use either a plain or sweet short crust flan case to make this dessert, a perfect end to a meal in late May or early June.

To make the short crust flan case, sift the flour and salt together in a bowl. Cut in the butter and then rub the mixture lightly together with your fingertips, lifting it to incorporate plenty of air until it resembles breadcrumbs. Then, using a palette knife, mix in enough water to bind the mixture to a dough and work it into a ball. Wrap and cool in the refrigerator for 20 minutes before using.

For the sweet short crust version, rub the flour and butter together until well combined and crumbly, but do not overwork. Stir in the salt and sugar, and then the egg and enough iced water to bind. Wrap and cool in the refrigerator for 20 minutes before using.

To bake blind, flour the work-top and lightly roll out the pastry. Line a greased tart tin 20–25 cm/8–10 inches in diameter. Prick the pastry all over, line with greaseproof paper, weight down with ceramic baking beans (dried beans will do, and can be stored and re-used for the same purpose), and bake blind, or empty of filling, for 8 to 10 minutes in an oven pre-heated to 200°C/400°F/gas mark 6.

Cream the cheese and sugar until soft, then stir in the cream until well blended and beat in 3 of the egg whites. Whisk the 3 remaining egg whites in a separate bowl and fold them into the creamed mixture, together with the elderflowers.

Spoon the cream into the pastry case, tap it hard on the work-top to settle the mixture and bake in a moderate oven, about 160°C/325°F/gas mark 3, for 40 minutes or until the mixture has just set. It is

serves 6 to 8

Short crust flan case
250 g/8 oz plain flour
1 scant teaspoon salt
125 g/4 oz unsalted butter, chilled and diced
approx 6 tablespoons chilled water

Sweet short crust flan case
250 g/8 oz plain flour
125 g/4 oz unsalted butter, chilled and diced
a pinch of salt
50 g/2 oz caster sugar
1 small egg, lightly beaten
iced water

For the filing
500 g/1 lb cream cheese *or* mascarpone
75–100 g/3–4 oz caster sugar
75 ml/3 fl oz whipping cream
6 egg whites
6–8 elderflower heads, flowers only
1 blind-baked short crust or sweet short crust flan case

important not to use a higher heat, as this will cause the protein in the egg white to set much too firmly.

Like most tarts and quiches, this is best served warm or at room temperature, but is also very tasty served cold the following day.

Cook's tip

If you have elderflower cordial (p.59), you can replace a third of the cream with it. And notice how whisking the egg white gives a slightly frothy texture to the tart, enhancing that of the elderflowers.

The perfect elderflower syllabub

This is the quintessential taste of England in early summer.

Put all the ingredients except the cream in a non-reactive saucepan, bring to the boil, remove from the heat and steep overnight. Whip the cream and gradually whisk in the strained liquid. Spoon into wine glasses and serve chilled with sponge fingers.

Cook's tip

You can flavour the syllabub with other aromatics and herbs as the season advances, even rose petals or lavender flowers.

serves 8

4–6 elderflower heads,
  depending on size
300 ml / ½ pint dry white wine
300 ml / ½ pint white grape juice
grated rind and juice of 2 lemons
a generous grating of nutmeg
200 g / 7 oz golden caster sugar
1 litre / 2 pints whipping *or*
  double cream

Gooseberry and elderflower fool

This recipe has the advantage that you can make it even if you don't have elderflowers to hand, as the gooseberries can be flavoured and sweetened either with fresh flower heads and sugar or with elderflower cordial.

Rinse the gooseberries (there is no need to top and tail them, as they will be sieved), then cook them gently until soft with the elderflowers, if these are in season; remove the flowers and sieve the gooseberries. Sweeten to taste, or add elderflower cordial if elderflowers are unavailable. Allow to cool and then fold in whipped cream or custard and chill until required.

This also makes a very good ice-cream, while elderflower cordial diluted with water makes an excellent sorbet, which can be served with the gooseberry crumble instead of the custard.

serves 4 to 6

1 kg/2 lb gooseberries
6 elderflower heads and caster
    sugar to taste *or* elderflower
    cordial (p.59) to taste
300 ml/½ pint double cream,
    whipped, *or* 450 ml/¾ pint
    home-made custard

Gooseberry and elderflower pudding

This is constructed in the same way as Summer
Pudding, a basin lined with sliced bread and filled
with fruit. But instead of a deep red berry fruit
dessert, the gooseberries make an interesting pale
version, which is enlivened with a garnish of herbs,
flowers and decorative edible leaves.

Top and tail the gooseberries and place them in a
saucepan with the water. Rinse and shake the
elderflowers, add them to the fruit and cook until the
gooseberries are soft. Sweeten to taste. Place a sieve
over a bowl and spoon in the gooseberries. Remove
the crust from the bread and cut into wedges to fit a
pudding basin, also cutting a circle for the base. Dip
the bread slices into the gooseberry syrup and line the
basin with it. Spoon in the gooseberry pulp and cover
with a layer of bread dipped in syrup, ensuring that all
the bread is well moistened. Cover, weight down and
refrigerate overnight.

Turn out onto a plate or shallow dish. Pour more
gooseberry syrup over it and decorate with edible
leaves and flowers. If you have sweet cicely or scented
geranium leaves, these can be dipped in the syrup and
used to line the pudding basin before you line it with
bread. When turned out, the leaves should be pressed
into the bread.

serves 6

1 kg/2 lb gooseberries
300 ml/½ pint water
3 elderflower heads
sugar to taste
6 or 7 slices from a large
    white loaf

Strawberry and elderflower jelly

Strawberries and elderflower have an affinity, I feel, and here I combine them in an impressive-looking dessert that is actually very easy to make. You will need a 1 kg/2 lb terrine to make this delicious dish. Using freshly ground black pepper as a seasoning for strawberries may seem surprising, but it enhances their flavour in the most distinctive way.

Soak the gelatine in a little water. Bring half the grape juice to the boil and steep the elderflowers in it for 2 to 3 hours. Bring half of the remaining juice to the boil, stir it into the softened gelatine until it has dissolved and then strain in the infused juice, together with sugar if needed, which is unlikely.

Take 200–250 g/about ½ lb of the softest strawberries and make a purée with them and the remaining grape juice in a blender, adding a little freshly ground black pepper. Sieve into a jug, cover and chill.

When the jelly has cooled, start the terrine by placing a layer of strawberries in the mould, covering with jelly and chilling until set. Add another layer of strawberries and jelly and, when this has set, continue in the same way until fruit and jelly have both been used up.

Chill until firm, turn out, slice and arrange on plates. Spoon the chilled strawberry sauce around the terrine, coarsely grind a little black pepper over the plate and decorate with fresh mint leaves.

serves 10

7 gelatine sheets *or* 7 teaspoons gelatine granules
750 ml/18 fl oz white grape juice
8 elderflower heads
1 kg/2 lb fresh strawberries, hulled and wiped
sugar to taste
black pepper

Raspberry and elderflower salad

This salad is so simple that it hardly requires a recipe. The delicate flavour of raspberries, sweet yet tart, and their velvety texture is subtly enhanced by the flavour of elderflowers. Simply put hulled raspberries in a bowl and sprinkle elderflower syrup (p.58) mixed with an equal volume of water over them. The water is important because it 'encourages' juice from the raspberries. If the season is right, and the idea appeals, scatter on a lacy pattern of tiny elderflowers before serving the fruit salad.

Apple and elderflower fritters

Elderflower fritters are a traditional dessert, but they also make an elegant accompaniment to a savoury dish such as griddled scallops, chicken breast or salmon fillet. If you are entertaining, however, it is much easier to serve them as a first course rather than later in the meal. Try the fritters plain, or with the addition of some finely chopped tart apple, a combination that goes especially well with fish.

Mix together the dry ingredients and then beat in the egg and liquid until you have a smooth, thick batter. Stir in the apple, lemon zest and juice, and finally fold in the elderflowers.

Heat the oil until a faint haze appears above it, but before it begins to smoke, and fry the fritters, scooping them off a dessertspoon, one at a time, until golden brown. Drain on paper towels and serve hot, as a garnish, or dusted with icing sugar as a dessert.

serves 4

200 g / 7 oz plain flour
a pinch of salt
2 teaspoons fast action yeast
1 egg
150 ml / 5 fl oz warm milk *or*
    75 ml / 2½ fl oz each cider
    and warm water
1 apple, peeled and finely diced
finely pared zest of 1 lemon
1–2 teaspoons lemon juice
12 elderflower heads, stripped
    from their stalks
sunflower, grapeseed or groundnut
    oil for frying
icing sugar for serving

Asparagus with elderflower hollandaise or mayonnaise

The combination of fresh green asparagus and a subtle hollandaise flavoured with elderflower is the perfect first course for a summer lunch. Asparagus also goes very well served cold with elderflower mayonnaise.

Trim the asparagus and boil until it is just tender. Drain and serve warm with the hollandaise or cold with the mayonnaise. To make a more substantial dish, serve freshly cooked new potatoes and carefully shelled soft-boiled eggs with the asparagus.

serves 2

500 g/1 lb green asparagus

Elderflower hollandaise

The slight hint of sweetness given by the elderflower cordial is a perfect complement to asparagus and also to shellfish.

Place 3 tablespoons of vinegar, the water, mace and peppercorns in a saucepan and boil to reduce to 1 tablespoon. Put the egg yolks in a bowl set over a pan of simmering water and beat them with a teaspoon of butter, a pinch of salt and a grating of pepper. Strain in the reduced vinegar and the elderflower cordial, remove the pan from the heat but keep the bowl over the hot water. Gradually whisk in the rest of the butter a little at a time, rather like making mayonnaise, until you have a smooth, glossy sauce. Taste to see whether a little more vinegar is required – this is unlikely if your elderflower cordial is nice and tart.

makes about 300 ml/½ pint

3 tablespoons elderflower vinegar
(p.33)
1 tablespoon water
1 blade of mace
4 peppercorns
3 egg yolks
1 teaspoon elderflower cordial
(p.59)
175 g/6 oz unsalted butter,
very soft
salt
pepper

Cook's tip

As with mayonnaise, you can make this in the food-processor, first blending the egg yolks, vinegar and seasoning, and then adding the butter, piece by piece. The blender is particularly useful if you are making double quantities or more.

Elderflower mayonnaise

If you want to intensify the elderflower flavour, you can also add a drop of elderflower cordial (p.58); the slight hint of sweetness goes well with asparagus, and also with shellfish.

Put the egg yolk in a bowl and season lightly. Initially, add the oil to the egg with a very sparing hand, literally drop by drop, beating in each addition of oil before adding the next. When the mixture starts to thicken, the oil can be added a little more liberally, but never more than about a tablespoon at a time. This too should be beaten until the mixture looks thick and glossy, but with no surface film of oil, before you add any more oil. When all the oil has been taken up, add more seasoning to taste and about 2 tablespoons of elderflower vinegar. If the mayonnaise seems very stiff and oily-looking, you can beat in a tablespoon of boiling water, which will emulsify and give a smooth, velvety texture.

makes about 300 ml / 1/2 pint

1 large egg yolk
300 ml / 1/2 pint sunflower or
    grapeseed oil
2–3 tablespoons elderflower
    vinegar (p.33)
salt
pepper

Cook's tip

The risk of curdling can be minimised if all the ingredients are all at room temperature. To make *sauce mousseline*, which is also a classic accompaniment for asparagus, fold in a stiffly beaten egg white.

Spring vegetables in elderflower jelly

Inspired by a recipe of Joel Robuchon's, here is a very pretty jelly to serve for a buffet lunch. It is worth making a large one, because, although it is easy to make, it is time-consuming as the vegetables should be cooked separately to retain their flavour.

The jelly is made first, and it is best to do this well enough in advance that you can cool, then chill it and so remove any fat easily.

Put all the ingredients in a large saucepan and cover with water. Add the wine, bring to the boil and skim all the impurities from the surface, then partially cover and simmer on the lowest possible heat until the pig's trotters are tender. This will take about three hours. Do not allow the stock to boil or it will turn cloudy. Carefully lift out the pig's trotters and the veal. These can be used in the finished dish and, in any case, are far too good to waste. Sieve the stock, cool and chill it until the fat has set, which you then remove.

Boil each vegetable until just tender, but make sure they retain their colour. Cooking them in an open pan, without the lid, helps. Drain and refresh them briefly under cold water, then put to one side.

Re-boil the stock – the perfectionist cook would at this stage clarify it by stirring in some lightly whisked egg white, simmering for 40 minutes, then carefully straining it through muslin and allowing it to cool again, but you may well decide that this is altogether too much trouble.

Shred the veal if using it, together with any meat you want to use from the pig's trotters. Layer all this with the vegetables in your terrine or glass bowl, then pour in the cool stock to the top and refrigerate until set.

Crème fraîche mixed with a little mustard and plenty of chives is good with this, as is a fresh tomato sauce with shredded basil.

serves 6–8

For the jelly

2 pig's trotters
1 kg/2 lb shin of veal
1/2 cm/1/4 inch ginger
thinly pared zest of 1 lemon
thinly pared zest of 1 orange
2 sticks of celery, chopped
a handful of watercress and
   parsley stalks
4 elderflower heads
1 shallot, quartered and each
   piece nailed with a clove
1 teaspoon of peppercorns
200 ml/7 fl oz white wine

For the vegetables

prepare a selection of about
1 kg/2 lb from the following,
using the 'baby' versions where
you can:

   leeks
   courgettes
   carrots
   purple or pink turnips
   fine green beans
   sugar snap peas
   fresh or frozen peas
   asparagus tips

Fennel flowers and borage

I love the versatility of fennel's flowers, seeds and feathery leaves, all of which have a powerful scent that never fails to remind me of the Mediterranean. The plant was naturalised in Britain many centuries ago, probably under the Romans, and is found in profusion almost everywhere it grows. Indeed, the Elizabethan writer John Gerard noted that, 'It is so well knowne amongst us, that it were but lost labour to describe the same.' For generations it has been used as a herbal remedy, especially as an aid to eyesight, as Longfellow suggests. Fennel seeds form part of the fragrant mixture taken at the end of a meal in India, which both freshens the breath and, one assumes, helps the digestion, while fennel tea makes a delicious end to a meal, especially at night in place of coffee.

The fennel used in the recipes that follow is *Foeniculum vulgarum*, the herb, not Florence fennel, also known as sweet fennel, which is a bulbous, sweet anise-flavoured white vegetable with fleshy overlapping leaves. We usually see this plant without its leaves, but in Italy it is generally sold complete with its leaves, which are used as a herb in cooking, notably in Sicily, where pasta and sardines are flavoured with copious quantities of fennel tops.

Herb fennel is easy to grow from seed and, because it is rather leggy, is best raised in borders or tubs rather than window boxes. The flowers are good in the

'The fennel with its yellow
  flowers
In an earlier age than ours,
Was gifted with the wondrous
  powers,
Lost vision to restore.'

Henry Longfellow,
Goblet of Life

kitchen, and also attractive in a jug as cut flowers, especially when mixed with others.

Much of my cooking with fennel flowers has been in Gozo, where I pick large bunches, together with borage and wild rocket, in early summer. I always bring a bag of fennel back to London, where the plant flowers in the late summer and early autumn, so that I can use its sweet, anise scent during the winter months.

I use fennel flowers with fish, poaching fillets in a scented broth, for example, and also find that it goes excellently with pork. In Italy, and particularly in Tuscany and Umbria, pork is often cooked in milk with fennel flowers and seeds, the milk gradually being transformed into a rich, caramel-coloured sauce flavoured with the juices from the meat. Fennel is also a classic Italian flavouring for sausages and salami, and potato salad made with a mayonnaise flavoured with fennel flowers is a delicious accompaniment to cold roast ham.

I also infuse fennel flowers in cream or milk to form the base of an unusual ice-cream or custard. You can use the infused cream for both sweet and savoury dishes. I use it as a sauce in the recipe for red mullet on p.78 and have also employed it, sweetened, as a filling for an orange cake. I also make a fennel syrup, to which I add lemon zest and juice as well as other fragrant herbs. This makes a refreshing drink when diluted with sparkling mineral water. Undiluted, it can be used as other syrups, principally as a flavouring for creams, custards and sauces, and also as a base for ice-creams and sorbets.

Fennel flower and lemon syrup

This syrup, which is best made with unwaxed and unsprayed lemons, is particularly delicious at breakfast when trickled over French toast, and also makes an excellent sorbet.

Thinly pare off the lemon zest and put it in a saucepan together with the fennel, thyme and geranium, verbena or linden blossom. Pour on the boiling water and simmer for 10 minutes before removing from the heat and leaving to infuse until cold. Halve and squeeze the lemons and add their juice to the saucepan, together with the sugar. Bring to the boil, ensuring that all the sugar has dissolved, simmer for 1 minute and remove from the heat. Strain when cool, pour into a clean wine bottle and keep in the refrigerator, where it can be stored for 3 to 4 months. For longer keeping at ambient temperatures, bottles of syrup should be sterilised – see p.59.

makes one 75 cl bottle

4 lemons
8 fennel flower heads
6 leaves of lemon-scented
    geranium or lemon verbena,
    or 6 linden blossom heads
a small sprig of lemon thyme
500 ml / 18 fl oz boiling water
500 g / 1 lb granulated sugar

Cook's tip

The lemon zest absorbs some of the syrup, retaining its herby flavour, so I keep it in an airtight box or bag in the freezer for using in a cake or ice-cream, snipping it into shreds with sharp scissors.

Red mullet fillets with fennel flower and orange sauce

Buttered spinach makes an excellent accompaniment to this simple but tasty dish.

Remove as many of the larger bones as you can from the fish, then rub it with half the orange zest and juice and season lightly with salt and pepper. Crumble one of the fennel flower heads over the fish, flesh side up, and leave for an hour for the flavours to mingle.

Brush a griddle or heavy cast-iron pan with olive oil and cook the fish fillets until done to your liking. Transfer them to a warm serving plate, raise the heat under the griddle or pan just long enough to heat the rest of the orange juice and zest and a tablespoon or so more olive oil. Crumble the remaining fennel flower over the fish and pour the dressing around it.

serves 2

1 large red mullet, scaled and
    filleted
juice and grated rind of 1 orange
2 fennel flower heads
extra virgin olive oil
salt
pepper

Roman calf's liver

This easily prepared dish is based on an ancient Roman recipe that soaks liver in milk and honey before cooking it, but requires a degree of planning, as the liver is marinated for anything up to 2 hours. I add dried fennel flowers to the marinade and also to the semolina in which I dip the liver before frying it.

Trim any piping from the liver. Gently warm the milk and honey just enough so that you can mix the two together and then remove from the heat. Add the calf's liver and half the fennel flowers and leave to marinate for at least half an hour and up to 2 hours.

Have your frying pan or griddle very hot and grease it lightly with butter. Mix the semolina and remaining fennel on a plate. Remove the liver from the liquid, allowing any excess to drip back into the bowl, and then dip it in the semolina so that both sides are

serves 2

2 thick slices of calf's liver
    weighing 150–200 g/
    5–7 oz each
100 ml/4 fl oz milk
1 tablespoon clear honey
2 tablespoons fennel flowers
4 tablespoons semolina
butter

coated. Fry or griddle for a few minutes on each side, according to how well-done you like liver.

I like to serve this with cucumber, an underrated vegetable that deserves to be used other than in salads. To prepare cucumber for cooking, peel and halve it, discarding the watery core. Cut it into finger-width strips and then into smaller batons. Cook them in a little butter until they are just beginning to turn brown.

Fennel-braised meat rolls

'Braciole' and 'braggioli' are the Italian and Maltese names for braised, stuffed meat rolls, usually pork or veal and pork. They are often served with a tomato sauce, but when I flavour them with fennel I like to serve a light white wine gravy so as not to smother the herb's delicate aroma.

Roll out the meat slices between cling film until thin. Place a piece of pork on each piece of veal. Mix the pepper, fennel, parsley, cheese and garlic, then spread on the pieces of veal. Roll the meat, folding in the edges and tie with cotton. Heat the oil and fry the ham and onion in it for a few minutes, then brown the meat rolls all over. Add the bay leaves and pour on the wine, scraping up any cooking residues. Bring to the boil, cover and cook on a low heat for 2 to 2½ hours, or bake in the oven at 150°C/300°F/gas mark 3 for about the same time. Add a little water or more wine if the dish shows signs of drying out. Serve with chunky pasta, mashed potatoes or rice.

serves 6 to 8

500 g/1 lb each thinly sliced
  veal and pork escalopes
black pepper
2 tablespoons fennel flowers
75 g/3 oz parsley, finely chopped
100 g/4 oz pecorino, grated
4 garlic cloves, crushed with a
  little salt
2 tablespoons extra virgin olive oil
100 g/4 oz raw ham, *pancetta*,
  salt pork or bacon, diced small
1 onion, thinly sliced
3 bay leaves
300 ml/½ pint full-bodied white
  wine

Slow roast pork with rice and fennel flowers

You can use belly, shoulder or knuckle of pork for this dish, but make sure it has a reasonable amount of both fat and skin and that the meat is in a single piece. The leaner cuts are not suitable because they tend to dry out. One of the rare breeds of pig, such as Gloucester Old Spot or Middle White, is best, as the meat is nicely marbled with fat.

Ensure the pork skin is well-scored before you start cooking. Your butcher is more likely to have the sharper knife, so it is probably best to ask him to do this for you.

Cut the garlic into slivers and push them into the slits in the skin and fat, as close as possible to the flesh but still within the fat.

Stir the syrup, zest and lemon juice together and rub the resulting mixture over the meat, which can be left overnight to absorb the flavours or put straight into the oven, together with the fennel flowers, once you have covered the roasting tin tightly with foil. Start it off for 15 minutes at 200°C/400°F/gas mark 6, then turn the heat down to 150°C/300°F/gas mark 3 and cook for 2 to 3 hours.

Remove from the oven and add the rice to the roasting pan, together with twice its volume of liquid, whether in the form of wine, water or stock, as well as the capers. You can also add a few almonds and raisins if you like. Season lightly with salt and pepper. Replace the foil and return the roasting tin to the oven. Cook for another hour or so, then check it again. You may need to add a little more liquid, as the finished dish should be moist and the rice soft rather than *al dente*. Continue cooking until the meat is tender enough to be eaten with a spoon.

serves 4 to 6

1 kg/2 lb pork
2 cloves garlic
3 tablespoons fennel flower and
   lemon syrup (p.77)
pared zest of 1 lemon
2 tablespoons lemon juice
6 or 8 fennel flower heads, plus
   extra for garnish
300 g/10 oz long-grain rice
300 ml/½ pint water, stock or
   white wine
2 tablespoons well-rinsed capers
salt
pepper

Fennel flower and cheese biscuits

Home-made cheese biscuits are simple to make, and
your guests will be very impressed that you have
baked them yourself. Using the same proportions, you
can make up a much larger batch of the mixture and
freeze several cylinders of dough for use when needed.

Rub the butter and flour together, stir in the cheese,
flowers and seeds, and add a little water to bind to a
firm dough. Roll out to the thickness of a £1 coin
and stamp out 5 cm/2 inch discs. Place on greased or
lined baking sheets and bake for 8–10 minutes at
180°C/350°F/gas mark 4. Cool on wire racks before
storing in an airtight container.

100 g/4 oz butter
100 g/4 oz plain flour
100 g/4 oz grated hard,
well-flavoured cheese such as
Parmesan, Cheddar or
Old Amsterdam
1 tablespoon fennel flowers
1 teaspoon fennel seeds, fresh
or dried

Cook's tip

To prepare in advance, roll the raw mixture into a cylinder, wrap well
and freeze. You can then cut off slices for baking as and when you
need them.

Orange and fennel flower sorbet

Put the flowers, sugar and water in a saucepan, heat
gently until the sugar has dissolved and then bring to
the boil and simmer for a few minutes. Remove from
the heat and allow the flowers to infuse for 20
minutes or so. Strain the syrup into the orange juice
and freeze.

If you have fresh fennel flowers, use them to decorate
the sorbet, otherwise a curl or two of finely pared
orange zest will do just as well.

serves 4

2 tablespoons fresh or
1 tablespoon dried fennel
flowers
150 g/5 oz granulated sugar
100 ml/4 fl oz water
600 ml/1 pint fresh orange juice

Borage flowers

I used to dismiss borage as simply a garnish for Pimm's, but now see it as a flower that has a useful role to play in the kitchen. Borage certainly adds colour to salads and other dishes, but it has little fragrance to speak of, other than a faint taste of cucumber, although it has long found favour with herbalists and cooks. In the sixteenth century John Gerard acknowledged the findings of Pliny and Dioscirides, who recognised that borage had a cheering effect, writing that, 'The leaves and floures of Borrage put into wine make men and women glad and merry, driving away all sadnesse, dulnesse and melancholy.' Borage was also thought to impart courage, and the flowers were given in wine to departing Crusaders, and also embroidered on banners taken into battle. Today, borage oil, extracted from the seeds, is sought after as an excellent source of Omega 3, and is sometimes sold as starflower oil.

Borage grows in wild profusion wherever it self-seeds, and it is said by gardeners that once you have borage, you will always have borage. The Victorians used it in a claret cup recipe, which could easily replace Pimm's as a favourite summer drink. To my mind, the Victorian concoction has considerably more personality.

'The sprigs of borage in wine are of known virtue to revive the hypochondriac and cheer the hard student.'

John Evelyn, *Acetaria*

Victorian claret cup

This is based on a recipe by Dorothy Hartley, who describes it as a perfect picnic drink. I have used her method, which is very sound, macerating the ingredients in the wine, chilling it well and only adding the sparkling water when the claret cup is served. This is a much better plan than having an open punch bowl with a large block of ice.

Mix all the ingredients together in a large jug or bowl and leave to stand, covered, in a cool place for an hour for the flavours to develop. Strain into a decanter and chill in the refrigerator, or stand the decanter in an ice-bucket, with both ice and water for rapid chilling.

To serve, pour some of the claret cup into glasses and top up with chilled sparkling water to taste, floating a borage flower on top.

10 ml/2 teaspoons sugar syrup
100 ml/4 fl oz amontillado sherry
25 ml/1 fl oz brandy
1/2 glass of maraschino or kirsch
a few drops of almond essence
thinly pared zest of 1 lemon
1 long strip of cucumber peel
1 head of borage flowers
one 75 cl bottle of claret

To serve
borage flowers
sparkling mineral water

Prawn and potato salad

Miss Hartley also comments on the attractiveness of borage flowers as a garnish in a salad together with scarlet nasturtium flowers, so, thinking about the ingredients that go well with cucumber, I decided to use borage flowers in a shellfish and potato salad. Using sweet cold water prawns that are already peeled, this makes a quick and easy first course. Jersey Royals, Charlottes or La Ratte are the tubers of choice for a potato salad.

Boil the potatoes until tender, drain and slice them quite thickly into a bowl when they are cool enough to handle. Mix in the cucumber, mayonnaise, prawns and half the flowers. Line two plates with salad leaves and heap the potato and prawn salad in the middle. Decorate with the remainder of the borage flowers.

serves 2

6 salad potatoes
half a cucumber, peeled, seeded and diced
2 or 3 tablespoons good mayonnaise
150 g/5 oz peeled prawns
two dozen borage flowers
salad leaves or baby spinach

Borage oil

Blue is not a colour usually associated with food, and encountering it when eating is something of a surprise. I like a little culinary shock from time to time and have developed this extraordinary blue oil to spoon onto creamy pale soups. It is best with chilled potato-based soups of the vichyssoise type. I make one with peeled cucumbers gently cooked in olive oil, chives and potatoes, blended to a pale creamy smoothness, faintly flecked with green.

3 tablespoons borage flowers,
the blue petals only
1/4 teaspoon sea salt
6 tablespoons sunflower oil

Put the petals in a mortar with a pinch of sea salt, which helps to 'grip' the pestle, and pound the petals to a paste. Gradually add the oil, ensuring that the mixture is well amalgamated. Mix it again before serving. You can either spoon it onto the soup or squeeze it through a plastic bottle, depending on the quantity you make and the effect you want to produce.

Borage pesto

It is only a small step from oil to pesto. If you can gather and pick over enough borage flowers, this is certainly worth trying. I have never been able to resist using it immediately, so do not know how well it retains its colour. Proceed exactly as you would for a traditional pesto made with basil, but use sunflower oil instead of extra virgin olive oil, as the flavour is milder and allows the faint flavour of the borage to come through, while too green an olive oil, unlike the more neutral sunflower oil, will distort its vivid blue colour.

What to serve with the pesto? White pasta and red cherry tomatoes? Steamed cod and beetroot salsa? A risotto flecked with chopped tomatoes and flakes of Parmesan?

Maltese widow's soup

I came across another use for borage in Malta, where the flowers grow in abundance wild along stone walls and it is traditional to strew it on bowls of 'widow's soup', *soppa tal-armla*. This is a substantial vegetable soup, almost a stew, in which a small fresh farm-made cheese called *gbejniet* is also served.

This recipe, suitable for widows, married couples, bachelors or anyone else you happen to invite for lunch, is based on the version in the Caruana Galizia sisters' excellent book on the food of the Maltese islands. It is a very useful dish if you find yourself cooking for vegetarians.

Gbejniet are small, soft, fresh cheeses, still made on a few farms in Malta and Gozo, for which a few slices from a log of goat's cheese can be substituted . Traditionally, only green and white vegetables are used in this soup. If you cannot find kohlrabi, a small turnip can be used instead.

Cook the onions and potatoes in the butter and oil until the onions begin to turn translucent and then stir in the rest of the vegetables. Cover with about 1 litre/2 pints water and simmer for 1 1/2 to 2 hours. When the soup is ready to serve, poach the eggs in it, then add the cheeses, including the ricotta, as well as the borage flowers and seasoning. For each serving, carefully transfer the eggs and cheese to hot soup bowls, then spoon in the vegetables and broth. Add extra borage flowers for decoration.

If you wish, you can add borage leaves early on, as a substitute for some of the spinach or lettuce, or simply as an additional vegetable. Crusty bread, hard on the outside, tender and chewy inside, is the perfect companion to this nourishing soup.

serves 4 to 6

2 onions, sliced
50 g/2 oz butter with a little
    extra virgin olive oil
2 potatoes, peeled and diced
200 g/7 oz cauliflower florets
200 g/7 oz baby spinach
1 celery stick, trimmed and sliced
1 kohlrabi, peeled and diced
2 cos lettuces, outer leaves
    removed, the heart sliced
1 curly endive, chopped
400 g/14 oz fresh peas, shelled
    weight
4 to 6 eggs
4 to 6 *gbejniet*
50–75 g/2–3 oz ricotta
a small bunch of borage
sea salt
black pepper

Fresh pasta with borage, hyssop and angelica

This is based on a dish we used to enjoy in Italy when staying with friends who had a large and varied organic garden.

Hyssop is one of the few herbs that cannot be bought easily and it is well worth growing. Its fragrance and slight bitterness are perfect with tomatoes, and here it combines with the subtle scents of borage and angelica. If angelica is not available, chervil can serve as a substitute. The tomato in this recipe should be subtle and light, so use peeled and diced fresh tomatoes, home-made tomato sauce or, at a pinch, *passata de pomodoro* or chopped canned plum tomatoes. Tomato purée adds too concentrated a flavour.

While the pasta is cooking, shred the prosciutto and put it in the frying pan with the butter and the hyssop and warm through for 30 seconds or so, without cooking the ham. Just before serving, stir in the angelica, the borage flowers and the tomato, and then stir in with the drained pasta. The angelica and borage should be added at the last minute or their elusive essences will evaporate instead of being captured by the butter. Serve in warmed soup plates.

serves 2

2 slices prosciutto
a nut of butter
10–12 hyssop leaves
2 heaped tablespoons fresh
　angelica stalk, finely sliced
2 teaspoons *passata di pomodoro*,
　fresh tomato sauce or strained,
　canned plum tomatoes
a handful of borage flowers
200 g / 7 oz home-made farfalle
　or other fresh pasta

Borage and spring onion frittata

This is an adaptation of a favourite Italian dish and makes an excellent quick lunch or supper or an appealing first course; it needs no salt because of the Parmesan.

Chop the green and white of the onions separately and cook first the white and then the green in a little oil in a heavy non-stick pan. Break in the eggs and mix them in the pan. Add several handfuls of freshly grated Parmesan. Mix all the ingredients together and then, just before the egg is cooked to your liking, stir in the borage flowers. The cheese makes this a very rich dish and the result is not flat, as a frittata usually is, but instead resembles scrambled eggs.

serves 3 to 4

2 bunches spring onions, trimmed and rinsed
extra virgin olive oil or grape seed oil
6 large eggs
100 g / 4 oz Parmesan cheese
a generous handful of borage flowers
pepper

Lavender

English lavender – *Lavandula vera, L. angustifolia, L. officinale* – is the most fragrant of all lavenders, the most highly prized for the quality of its essential oils, which are used in the perfume industry. Less hardy varieties, particularly French lavender, *L. stoechas*, are also used for making oils and perfumes, but they do not have the deep, piercing fragrance of English lavender. They look slightly different too, somewhat like elongated pine cones, with distinctive purple bracts at the tip. Ironically, English lavender is the flower grown in Provence for the perfume industry.

I am sorry to say that rows of lavender bushes stretched out beneath a Mediterranean sky were not what first inspired me to use flowers in the kitchen. It was a rather more prosaic scene – my parents' garden in Derbyshire during a particularly hot summer that brought the roses out in unimaginably large fragrant blooms and also produced piercingly fragrant, deep purple flower spikes on a large bush of English lavender, which I immediately wanted to capture as a flavour.

Lavender has an 'androgynous' scent – both savoury and sweet, with distinct hints of the herbal and medicinal about it, more so than, say, roses, whose scent is much more 'feminine'. The quality of its scent and flavour is more akin to that of rosemary and thyme, which makes it suitable for savoury dishes. However when you marry the flowers with sugar,

'Good master, let's go to that house, for the linen looks white, and smells of lavender, and I long to lie in a pair of sheets that smell so.'

Izaak Walton,
The Compleat Angler, 1682

cream, chocolate or butter, a whole new world of unusual desserts open up.

I quickly decided that lavender would enhance lamb just as well as rosemary does, and was determined to find a way of translating its haunting fragrance into a flavour that I could use in my cooking. The simplest way to do this is to use the lavender flowers as a herb, with lamb chops, roast lamb, veal or poultry. Pushing a few lavender spikes under the skin of a chicken is a method I picked up in California twenty years ago from Judy Rodgers at Zuni Café, when she was using a variety of herbs to perfume chicken. Lemon-scented herbs work well, as does lavender. Try it with chicken breasts, as well as the whole bird. Quail are also rather fabulous cooked with lavender, while Chez Panisse in Berkeley serves a delicious lavender honey ice-cream with an apple tart.

In *Recettes de Cuisine de Vieil Alger* by Aïcha Zadek, there is a recipe for lavender couscous, *couscous bel halhal*. She uses '*une assez grande quantité*' to perfume and colour the couscous, which turns black and is eaten with sugar rather than as an accompaniment to savoury dishes. Madame Zadek suggests gathering the wild lavender at the end of winter, on the Friday walk with the children. In order to be able to cook this dish outside the lavender season, she advises mixing the lavender flowers with the couscous, steaming it just once, then spreading it all out to dry for 4 or 5 days, after which it can be stored in a dry place in an airtight container for use later in the year. In Europe, of course, lavender flowers in the summer and we store it for use in the winter. Following the same principle, I have put dried lavender flowers in a jar of rice and then used it to make a delicately scented and flavoured rice pudding. These two ideas made me wonder whether there might be an affinity between lavender and wild rice, and that led me to develop a wild rice pilaff with lavender and toasted almonds (p.118), a dish that goes especially well with pheasant, which can sometimes be rather dull.

Traditionally, lavender has not been seen as a culinary

herb, and its use in the kitchen is relatively recent. It has always been used to scent and soothe, but more in the sense of the quotation that opens this chapter, to perfume linens and gloves, to scent the steam in an iron, to rub on one's temple at times of stress. Indeed, many of the lavender vinegar recipes from the early part of the twentieth century were intended to be used as 'toilet vinegars', in much the same way as we use *eau de toilette* today.

There are a few French recipes employing lavender that might be considered classics, such as *crème brulée à la lavande, glace à la lavande*, and a number of dishes that use lavender honey, including *magret de canard au miel de lavande*. Lavender goes surprisingly well with fish, especially when cooked in the Mediterranean style, for example red mullet or sea bass grilled over lavender stalks – every bit as good as fennel, and you can also use a few of the flowers to perfume the flesh from inside (p.78).

It is worth noting, of course, that the classic fragrant mixture *herbes de Provence* includes crushed lavender flowers and that *ras el hanout*, the famous Moroccan spice mixture, also contains powdered lavender as well as rose petals.

Lavender has therapeutic properties and professional advice should sought before using it in medicinal quantities. A few people are highly allergic to lavender, so it may worth enquiring of your guests before serving a dish that includes lavender.

The quantities used in the following recipes are small, but sufficient to perfume and flavour the dishes.

Lavender salt

Salt has no volatile oils and flavour compounds to combine with other ingredients, so you cannot make a flavoured salt by 'infusing' it with another ingredient as you can a flavoured sugar. Celery salt, for example, is made by grinding dried celery seeds with salt, and this is the method to use if you want lavender salt, which cannot be made by simply burying a few lavender sprigs in a jar of salt.

Use about one part flowers to about ten parts coarse sea salt, which responds best to grinding. The flowers need to be absolutely dry or they will cake with the salt; I always put a few grains of rice in the bottom of the jar to help keep the flavoured salt dry.

Lavender salt is an unusual and subtle flavour-enhancer to freshly cooked vegetables, served warm rather than hot. Green or white asparagus, new potatoes tossed in butter and a soft-boiled egg, all dusted with a little lavender salt are a gustatory delight. Sprinkle lavender salt on cod fillets cooked in olive oil with garlic or use it to season duck breasts before grilling them.

Toasted nut and lavender crunch

Dhukka is a fabulous Egyptian condiment, combining ground toasted hazelnuts, sesame seeds, coriander and cumin seeds, thyme, salt and pepper. I have made two versions using lavender, in one replacing the thyme with lavender flowers, which can be used as a savoury crust for fish fillets.

In the second version I replace the thyme with lavender and the salt with Demerara or golden granulated sugar and use the mixture in crumble toppings for fruit, as well as sprinkled on an iced chocolate cake. You can also use it round the sides of a cake, which should first be brushed with a glaze or jelly to hold the crumbly mix.

200 g / 8 oz hazelnuts, toasted
100 g / 4 oz sesame seeds, toasted
100 g / 4 oz golden granulated sugar
2 teaspoons lavender flowers
1 tablespoon cumin, lightly toasted
1 tablespoon coriander seeds, lightly toasted
a pinch of freshly ground black pepper

Toasted nut and lavender crunch /continued

A wonderful sundae can be made with a scoop of vanilla ice-cream, over which you spoon palm syrup and then sprinkle the sweet toasted lavender crunch. And, because lavender and chocolate have a real affinity, it also goes very well with chocolate sauce poured over the ice-cream.

First, dry the lavender flowers for a few hours, otherwise the oil and moisture will cause the rest of the mixture to turn into a paste when ground.

Put the hazelnuts in a clean coffee-grinder and grind briefly, until the nuts are broken up, then add the rest of the ingredients and again grind just until the mixture is granular and of approximately even size, rather than a powder or a paste.

For the savoury version, use 2 teaspoons of salt instead of the sugar.

Store in an airtight jar in a cupboard, and it will stay fresh for up to 6 months. You can also make a large quantity and store in the freezer in bags, in which case it will keep for a year – until the next lavender season.

Lavender ratafia

This brandy-based cordial is excellent in cakes and added to warm sauces for puddings. Try making a champagne cocktail with the sugar-cube soaked in lavender ratafia instead of cognac – it makes a subtle and intriguing drink.

Shake the lavender, strip off the flowers and put them in a preserving jar. Pour in the brandy, seal and leave for 2 to 3 months in a dark place. Strain the brandy into a bowl and stir in the sugar syrup. Bottle and label. Like any liqueur, this ratafia keeps almost indefinitely.

makes about 50 cl/18 fl oz

10 lavender heads
50 cl/18 fl oz brandy
200 g/7 oz sugar, or to taste,
    dissolved to a syrup in 2 to 3
    tablespoons of water

Lavender jelly

Serve this as a stunning garnish for summer fruit salads, or as the base for a lively sundae or other exotic dessert. Food colouring is essential if you want a jewel-like true lavender shade.

Break up the gelatine and soak it in a glass of cold water. When it is soft, drain off the water and stir the gelatine into the boiling water. When the gelatine has dissolved, stir in the lavender syrup and check the flavour. Add more sugar and a dash of lemon juice if you think it needs it. Carefully add a drop or two of food colouring and, once the liquid is cool, pour it into a fairly shallow container and chill until set. Turn out the jelly and cut it into whatever shapes take your fancy.

This jelly looks particularly attractive with a salad of green-fleshed melons or a mixture of green fruit.

Cook's tip

Violets, rose petals and saffron can be also be used to make colourful jellies to decorate other desserts, while a pale elderflower jelly goes very well with strawberries, gooseberries or apricots.

will garnish a dessert for 8–10

4 leaves gelatine
300 ml / ½ pint boiling water
100 ml / 4 fl oz lavender syrup
    (p.31)
lemon juice and additional sugar
    to taste
purple food colouring

Apricot and lavender jam

Ripe Provençal apricots are in the market when English lavender is still in bloom. You can also make this jam in winter using dried apricots and dried lavender.

Have your clean jars heating in the oven while you prepare the fruit. Peel and core the apple, then dice it very finely. Halve the apricots, discarding the stones, and chop the fruit very small. There is no need to remove the skin unless it is loose. Put the apple in a saucepan with 150–200 ml / 5–7 fl oz of water and the lavender sprigs. Cook until the fruit is soft and then add the apricots. Cook until these too are soft and the apple has disintegrated.

Strain the juices into your jam-pan and add the preserving sugar. Heat gently until the sugar has dissolved, boil the syrup for two minutes and then add the fruit. Stir well, bring back to the boil, skimming any foam that gathers on the surface, and boil until setting point is reached. This will take 3 or 4 minutes.

Take the pan off the heat, remove the lavender stalks and fill the hot jars with the jam. Cover with waxed paper discs and screw-top lids or cellophane covers. Label and store in a cool dark place.

makes about 1.5 kg/3 lb

1 Bramley apple or other tart apple
  such as Granny Smith
1 kg / 2 lb ripe but firm apricots
6 sprigs lavender
750 g / 1½ lb preserving sugar

Lemon and lavender curd

Lemon and lavender combine superbly and this curd makes a fabulous filling for tarts, which you can then dust with a little of the lavender crunch mixture (p.91).

Grate the rinds and squeeze the juice from the lemons, then put them both in a double saucepan. Cut the butter into small cubes and add it to the pan with the lightly beaten eggs and the sugar and lavender. Stir until the sugar has dissolved and continue cooking on a low heat, stirring the mixture until it thickens. Remove the lavender heads and pot in small, clean, dry jars that you have warmed in the oven. Cover immediately, label, refrigerate and use within 3 to 4 weeks. If you want a stronger flavour, you can add a sprig of fresh lavender to each jar just before potting.

makes about 600 g/1½ lb

This recipe uses uncooked eggs

4 large lemons with good skins
8 egg yolks or 4 whole eggs
150 g/5 oz unsalted butter
350 g/12 oz golden granulated
    sugar
6 lavender heads

Lemon and lavender marmalade

A thick skin is the secret of good marmalade, as it contains the bitterness that gives marmalade its bite. Seville oranges, pink or ordinary grapefruit and thick-skinned lemons are all ideal for marmalade-making. Lemons are available all year round and those from the southern hemisphere coincide with the lavender season, allowing you to use fresh flowers. To make winter marmalade, when Seville oranges are in season, use dried flowers. On balance, I find lavender and lemon a better combination than lavender and orange.

Scrub the lemons well, rinse and quarter them. Gently pull out the sections holding the juicy cells, pick these away from the skin and put them in a heavy saucepan. Place the skin and all the pips into a piece of muslin, tie it up and add to the saucepan; if you have tea filter bags, these are ideal for marmalade-making. Halve the pieces of skin lengthways and then slice very thinly with a sharp knife. Place the fruit in the saucepan, just cover with water and cook gently – covered – for

makes about 2 kg/4 lb

6 lemons with unblemished skins
water – see recipe
granulated or preserving sugar –
    see recipe
4 to 6 sprigs lavender

Lemon and lavender marmalade /continued

2 hours or until the skin is soft and translucent.

Remove from the heat and carefully transfer the contents of the saucepan to a container that will go on your scales. Weigh the pulp and liquid. Return the mixture to the saucepan and add an equal weight of granulated or preserving sugar and the lavender. Heat until the sugar has dissolved and then boil vigorously until setting point is reached, which can take anything from 15 to 40 minutes.

Fill hot, clean jars right to the top, seal and label.

Cook's tip

Tea filter bags have a variety of uses in the kitchen. They come in handy when making marmalade and also *bouquets garnis*. When cooking with flowers, they are useful for keeping the petals separate from other ingredients while allowing their flavour to infuse the dish. It is well worth keeping a packet for general kitchen purposes.

Lavender ice-cream

Lavender ice-cream is delicious on its own, but can also be served with fresh raspberries or, for real decadence, with chocolate sauce.

Grind 150 g / 5 oz of the sugar and the lavender buds with a mortar and pestle or a clean coffee-grinder until they are thoroughly blended. Stir into the milk and bring to the boil. Beat the cream and egg yolks together in a bowl and pour the lavender-flavoured milk into it, stirring constantly. Return the mixture to the pan and cook very gently until it just coats the back of a spoon, but take care not let it boil or the eggs will curdle. Allow to cool and then freeze, either in an ice-cream maker or in the freezer.

Crystallise the lavender flowers by following one of the methods on p.37.

serves 6 to 8

This recipe uses uncooked eggs

175 g / 6 oz granulated or caster sugar
1–2 teaspoons fresh lavender buds, plus extra heads for decoration
300 ml / ½ pint full-cream milk
7 egg yolks
300 ml / ½ pint single cream

Lavender crème brulée

I hesitate to give this recipe, as I believe that the best crème brulée is a plain one. A crème brulée made with fruit is an abomination – the acid in the fruit turns the cream and the whole dish becomes like stodgy cheesecake instead of an ethereal cream, but infused creams do work and jasmine tea crème brulée can be divine.

Bring the cream and lavender to the boil. Beat the egg yolks and caster sugar in a bowl set over hot water or in the top of a double boiler and pour the scalded cream onto the mixture, beating continuously. Heat the custard, stirring constantly until it thickens. Remove from the heat and stir until cool. Remove the lavender, pour the custard into ramekins and chill until set. Mix the Demerara sugar and lavender crunch mixture and sprinkle an even layer on each ramekin. Caramelise it under the grill or, if you own such a toy, with a kitchen blow-torch. Chill again until required.

To make a jasmine tea crème brulée, replace the lavender with a teaspoon of jasmine tea, and sieve the mixture before pouring into ramekins.

serves 6

This recipe uses uncooked eggs

600 ml / 1 pint double cream
4 sprigs lavender
6 egg yolks
50 g / 2 oz caster sugar
100 g / 4 oz Demerara sugar
2 tablespoons lavender crunch
(p.91)

White chocolate lavender truffles

Add half the lavender heads to the cream and bring to
the boil. Remove from the heat and, while leaving it
to infuse for 5 minutes, break the chocolate into
pieces and place them in a bowl. Then strain the
cream and lavender mixture over the chocolate; the
heat of the cream should be sufficient to melt the
chocolate – if it isn't, simply stand it over a pan of hot
water. Stir the mixture and, when it's completely
smooth, remove from the heat and beat vigorously.
When the bowl is cool, put it in the refrigerator.

Strip the flowers from the remaining lavender heads,
which can be dried but should still be reasonably
fresh. Place the flowers and the sugar in an absolutely
clean coffee-grinder and grind until you have
powdered lavender sugar.

Scoop the chilled chocolate mixture into 12 portions,
roll each one on a plate or marble slab, smooth to a
truffle shape and then roll them in the flavoured and
scented sugar.

To make rose truffles, omit the lavender and add 2 to
3 teaspoons of rosewater to the cream as you boil it.
Roll the white truffle in icing sugar or melted white
or dark chocolate and decorate with a piece of
crystallised rose, which you can buy in good
confectioners or bakery suppliers.

makes 12

6 lavender heads
100 ml/4 fl oz double cream
100 g/4 oz white chocolate
4 tablespoons granulated sugar

Lavender pralines

Any recipe that requires sugar to be cooked to the
caramel stage is slow, hot work, so it is worth getting
up early to make these if you don't want to sweat over
a hot stove on a summer's day. The idea of substituting
lavender for nuts came to me when making the
lavender nut crunch on p.91 and I then wondered
about stirring the flowers into hard crack caramel,
letting it harden on a marble slab and crushing the

makes 2 to 3 dozen

300 g/10 oz caster sugar
150 g/5 oz light muscovado sugar
300 ml/½ pint double cream
2 teaspoons lavender flowers
2 tablespoons butter
1 teaspoon pure vanilla essence
a pinch of salt

result or serving it as a sweetmeat. And so from there to pralines, an altogether more toothsome confection.

Cook the sugar and cream over a medium heat in a heavy saucepan or frying pan until the sugar has dissolved, stirring just enough to prevent sticking and without scraping down the sides. As soon as the mixture is boiling rapidly, add the flowers, butter and salt. Let the mixture reach 165°C/325°F on a sugar thermometer, remove from the heat, stir in the vanilla and beat vigorously with a wooden spoon for 2 minutes.

When the mixture begins to thicken and cool, spoon it into rounds on wax paper and leave to cool completely. Wrap each praline individually and store them in an airtight container.

Caramel pears with lavender

I have also made this recipe with rosemary sprigs and flowers, and the result is equally exquisite.

Put the pears in a heavy saucepan and add the sugar, a tablespoon of water and three sprigs of lavender. Cover with a tight-fitting lid, cook gently until the pears are tender, which may take from 15 to 45 minutes depending on variety and ripeness, and transfer them to individual dishes or a serving bowl. Remove the lavender from the pan, bring the syrup to the boil and cook until it begins to caramelise. Add the cream, bring back to the boil, cook until the crème fraîche thickens and pour over or around the fruit. Spike the pears with lavender sprigs and serve.

serves 6

6 pears, peeled and cored
6 tablespoons Demerara or light
    muscovado sugar
3 sprigs lavender, plus 6 for
    decoration
4 heaped tablespoons full-fat
    crème fraîche

Lavender sorbet with blueberry soup

This is one of my favourite summer desserts, and I like to ring the changes with it by combining camomile sorbet with peach soup, elderflower sorbet and strawberry soup or linden flower sorbet accompanied by a delicate apricot soup.

Using fresh lavender makes an appreciable difference in sorbets. The aromatic oils fade fairly quickly, and if you use dried lavender the flavour tends to be somewhat flattened, bearing in mind that chilling also reduces its flavour.

Make a syrup with the water and sugar and bring to the boil. Peel off the lemon zest, add it and the lavender flowers to the boiling syrup and leave to infuse for several hours or overnight. Stir in the lemon juice, strain the infusion, cool and freeze. Using less sugar will give you a grainier sorbet, while more sugar will make it smoother.

Put all but a handful of the blueberries, the grape and the lemon juice, sugar and water in a food-processor and blend until smooth. Pour into chilled soup plates and add a scoop of sorbet. The whole blueberries are added for garnish; fresh lavender flowers or mint leaves can also be used.

serves 6

Sorbet
600 ml / 1 pint water
400 g / 14 oz granulated sugar
zest and juice of 1 lemon
1–2 teaspoons fresh lavender
  flowers

Soup
400 g / 14 oz blueberries
300 ml / ½ pint red grape juice
juice of half a lemon
2–3 tablespoons sugar
300 ml / ½ pint chilled water

Apple, almond and lavender jelly

Flower jellies are one of the tastiest of all tea-time treats, and they also make good presents. I don't advocate keeping them for longer than a year, but I am always surprised at how long the flower fragrance lasts. I once served some that was over two years old and, although the colour had deepened, the flavour was still fresh. See the note on p.42 about which apples to use when making jelly.

Before you start to prepare the fruit, put your jam jars to warm in the oven. Chop the apples – peel, core, pips and all – and put them in a large saucepan together with half the lavender wrapped in a muslin bag or tea filter. Cover with water and cook until the fruit is tender, mashing to extract as much juice and flavour as possible. Suspend a jelly bag or large scalded muslin cloth over a bowl, ladle in the fruit pulp and leave it to drip through overnight.

Measure out the juice and put it in a saucepan. Then weigh the sugar, allowing 500 g/1 lb of sugar for 600 ml/1 pint of juice, and add the rest of the lavender in another muslin bag. Cook gently until the sugar has dissolved and then bring to a rapid boil until setting point is reached – this will take about 20 minutes. Skim the surface and allow to stand for a few minutes before stirring in the almonds and removing the bag of lavender.

Put a lavender flower in each jar, fill with jelly, seal and label.

makes about 2.5 kg/5 lb

1.5 kg/generous 3 lb cooking apples, crab apples or windfalls
6 lavender heads, plus one sprig for each jar
granulated or preserving sugar – see recipe
75 g/3 oz blanched flaked almonds

Apricot and lavender fool

Apricots, cherries, blueberries and plums are the fruits that respond best to a breath of lavender fragrance. This fruit fool is summer encapsulated, but you can also make it in winter by soaking dried apricots and using lavender sugar – a cold, dull day will miraculously become much brighter.

Rinse the apricots and place them in a saucepan with the honey and 2 sprigs of lavender. Put the lid on the pan and simmer on a very gentle heat until the apricots are soft, then rub the pulp through a sieve and allow to cool for 20 minutes or so. Fold the mixture into the yoghurt or custard, sweeten to taste with more sugar, spoon into glasses and chill for a couple of hours. Meanwhile, rinse the remaining 6 sprigs of lavender, shake dry and roll them in the sugar. Put them somewhere very dry, perhaps the bottom of a recently switched off oven, and allow to become crisp. Serve the glasses of fool on saucers with a sprig of lavender as an edible decoration.

serves 6

750 g / 1½ lb apricots, stones removed
2 tablespoons lavender honey (p.111)
golden caster sugar – see recipe
6 sprigs lavender
300–400 ml / 10–14 fl oz thick Greek yoghurt or custard

Lavender shortbread

I developed this recipe when doing some menu consultancy for Garsington Opera, where the terrace was lined with lavender bushes and inspiration was not hard to find. This shortbread is excellent with ice-cream or sorbet, lavender or otherwise, and also with fruit fools, such as gooseberry, with which it was originally served.

Cream the butter and sugar, stir in the flour and add just enough water to make a stiff pastry. Roll out to about 1 cm/scant ½ inch thick and cut into fingers or rounds. Bake for 20 to 30 minutes at 165°C/325°F/ gas mark 3 and dust with caster sugar 5 minutes before removing from the oven. Cool on a wire rack.

makes about 30

100 g / 4 oz unsalted butter
75 g / 3 oz lavender sugar (p.28)
150 g / 6 oz plain flour, sifted
iced water, if required
caster sugar for dusting

Lavender and blueberry griddle cakes

If you want to make this recipe in winter, use dried blueberries and 50 g / 2 oz lavender sugar (p.29).

Heat a non-stick griddle or heavy frying pan. Sift the dry ingredients together and rub in the butter. Mix in the sugar, lavender and blueberries and finally stir in enough liquid to make a smooth, fairly soft dough. Roll or pat the dough flat and cut into rounds about ½ cm / ¼ inch thick with a scone-cutter.

Cook on the hot griddle for about 4 minutes on each side. It is important that you heat the griddle before starting, because once the acidic liquid mixes with the baking powder, the rising action begins and cooking must take place immediately; if it doesn't, the dough will toughen.

Serve warm with raspberry jam, or something plainer such as a clear apple jelly.

serves 6

350 g / 12 oz plain flour
3 teaspoons baking powder
a pinch of salt
150 g / 5 oz butter
50 g / 2 oz sugar
2 teaspoons lavender flowers
75 g / 3 oz fresh blueberries
about 100 ml / 4 fl oz yoghurt
   mixed with water or buttermilk

Lavender and almond crisps

Pre-heat the oven to 170°C / 325°F / gas mark 3.

Mix together the sugar and almonds and stir in the egg white to make a paste.

Line a baking tray with rice paper or a non-stick baking sheet and place teaspoonfuls of the mixture at regular intervals about 5 cm / 2 inches apart. Flatten the mixture slightly. Bake for 12 to 15 minutes until just firm. Switch off the oven and replace the tray of biscuits on the bottom shelf, leaving them for about 15 minutes or so to dry completely.

Remove from the oven and transfer the biscuits to wire racks to cool.

makes about 18

110 g / 4 oz lavender sugar
   (see p.29)
110 g / 4 oz ground almonds
1 large egg white, lightly beaten

Warm chocolate lavender cake

This recipe takes its inspiration from several sources, including a decadent cake prepared by the pastry chef in Michelle Bernstein's kitchen at Azul in the Mandarin Oriental Hotel, Miami. Just as rosemary goes well with chocolate, so too does lavender. This recipe should be made with a chocolate with at least 70 per cent cocoa solids

Butter six 100 ml ramekins and dust them with cocoa. Break up the chocolate, melt it in a bowl set over hot water and remove from the heat.

Set another bowl over hot water and beat the three whole eggs with the lavender sugar until pale and the mixture leaves ribbons when trailed from the whisk.

Whisk the egg whites with the caster sugar until firm. Carefully – and gradually – fold the melted chocolate, the egg yolk and egg white mixtures together. Spoon into the ramekins, put them in a roasting tin with a little water and place in an oven pre-heated to 165°C/325°F/gas mark 3 for 15 to 20 minutes, or one notch up for 12 to 15 minutes.

Remove from the oven and allow the cakes to cool in the ramekins for a few minutes until they begin to shrink from the edge. The mixture will rise during cooking, but will now begin to sink. Ease round the cakes with a knife and gently turn them out onto serving plates, which you might want to dust beforehand with icing sugar or cocoa.

A lavender sauce or custard goes well with these moist, light cakes, which should still be creamy right in the centre. The sauce is also very good with dark chocolate ice-cream.

serves 6

15 g / ½ oz unsalted butter
2 tablespoons cocoa powder
150 g / 5 oz chocolate
3 eggs plus 2 egg whites
5 scant dessertspoons lavender
    sugar (p.29)
2 teaspoons caster sugar

Lavender and almond sauce

Scald the milk with the lavender and remove from the heat. Break the marzipan into small pieces. Whisk the milk powder into the infused milk and stir in the marzipan. When the marzipan has dissolved, stir the sauce once more, strain and serve either warm or cold.

serves 6

200 ml/7 fl oz skimmed milk
1 teaspoon lavender flowers
150 g/5 oz marzipan
4 tablespoons skimmed milk
  powder

Double chocolate and lavender tarts

With both chocolate pastry and chocolate filling, these tarts will satisfy even the most ardent chocoholic. The filling should be made with good quality chocolate, that is to say one that has at least 70 per cent cocoa solids.

Rub the butter into the flour and cocoa and then stir in the sugar and egg yolk. Add iced water, if necessary, to bind to a pastry and leave to rest for half an hour, then roll out and line 4 pastry cases about 10–12 cm/ 4–5 inches in diameter.

Then, following the instructions on p.66, bake blind for 6 to 8 minutes at 180°C/350°F/gas mark 4, remove from the oven and leave to cool. You can make the pastry cases a day or so in advance, if this is more convenient.

Whisk the eggs and sugar until pale and much increased in volume. Break up the chocolate into a bowl set over a pan of hot water and melt it in the cream. Remove from the heat, beat in the butter and fold into the egg mixture.

Leave to cool, then spoon into the pastry cases and bake for 5 minutes in an oven pre-heated to 150°C/ 300°F/gas mark 2.

Serve dusted with icing sugar and decorated with some crystallised lavender flowers – see p.37.

makes 4

Pastry
50 g/2 oz unsalted butter
75 g/3 oz plain flour
sifted with
25 g/1 oz cocoa
1 tablespoon caster sugar
1 egg yolk
iced water

Filling
2 egg yolks
1 whole egg
50 g/2 oz lavender sugar (p.29)
50 ml/2 fl oz double cream
150 g/5 oz dark chocolate
25 g/1 oz unsalted butter,
  softened

Chocolate, lavender and almond biscuits

I find the combination of chocolate and lavender almost addictive, and there is now even a Belgian chocolate bar flavoured with lavender. Try these delicious biscuits as an alternative.

Cream the butter and sugar, and then beat in the egg, liquid and flour. Break up the chocolate and stir it, the almonds and the lavender into the mixture.

Flour your hands and scoop up walnut-size balls weighing about 15 g/1/2 oz and, spacing them well, place on two greased baking sheets. Press down with your fingers or a spatula to a diameter of about 7.5 cm/3 inches and bake for 12 to 15 minutes in an oven pre-heated to 180°C/350°F/gas mark 4. Remove from the oven, leave for a minute or two and then cool the biscuits on a wire rack.

makes 24

125 g/4 oz unsalted butter
125 g/4 oz golden caster sugar
1 egg
beaten with
2 tablespoons lavender ratafia
 (p.92) or Amaretto
175 g/6 oz plain flour
75 g/3 oz dark chocolate
75 g/3 oz flaked almonds
1–2 teaspoons lavender flowers

Cook's tip

If you want to make larger quantities, roll the biscuit dough into cylinders, wrap in cling film and freeze until required. Simply slice off as much as you need.

Apricot and lavender tea loaf

Another apricot and lavender combination, this cake is ideal for a summer tea and, not being too sweet, goes well with a leisurely Sunday brunch. You can also make it with ready-to-eat dried apricots, which do not need be soaked before cooking.

Soften the butter in a mixing bowl with a wooden spoon. Gradually work in the egg yolks, honey and lavender sugar, then add the whole egg and the cream, mixing until you have a smooth batter. Add the flour and salt, and fully incorporate into the batter, which should now be thick and smooth. Rinse, dry and stone the apricots. Cut one and a half into neat slices, for decoration, and dice the rest, which you add to the cake batter. Spoon into a greased or lined cake tin, about 25 x 9 cm/10 inches by 4 inches, decorate the top with the apricot slices and sprinkle with a little sugar so that the fruit will caramelise nicely on top.

Bake for 10 minutes in an oven pre-heated to 220°C/425°F/gas mark 7, then for a further 35 minutes at 200°C/400°F/gas mark 6. Allow the cake to cool in its tin and, if possible, leave until the next day for the flavours to develop.

serves 6

100 g / 4 oz butter, at room temperature
2 egg yolks
3 soup spoons clear honey
75 g / 3 oz granulated sugar
ground with
1 1/2 teaspoons fresh lavender flowers
100 ml / 4 fl oz double cream
1 egg
225 g / 8 oz self-raising flour
sifted with
1/2 teaspoon ground mace
a pinch of salt
6 or 7 firm but ripe apricots

Poached trout in spiced lavender jelly

One of the simplest and best lavender recipes in the medieval culinary repertoire comes from *Il Libro della Cucina del Secolo XIV*, edited by Francesco Zambrini. I particularly like it because, most unusually, the lavender is used in a savoury dish. A modern version of *poissons en gelée* is given in *La Gastronomie au Moyen Age*, a fabulous collection of 150 medieval Italian and French recipes tested, compiled and brought up to date by Françoise Sabban and her colleagues Odile Redon and Silvano Serventi. I have adapted the recipe further, because I prefer to use whole rather than ground spices and fresh rather than powdered ginger.

This is a summery dish, perfect for a buffet lunch or supper. Dr Sabban's recipe suggests individual rainbow trout, which makes for a most delicate dish, but you can also use a small sea trout. It is important to use whole fish as you need the skin and bone to make a stock firm enough to set to a jelly.

Make a *court bouillon* by bringing the wine, water and vinegar to the boil in a deep roasting tin or large fish kettle; skim if necessary and remove from the heat. Season the trout inside and out and wrap each one in a piece of clean cheesecloth or muslin to ensure that the fish does not break up.

When the *court bouillon* has cooled, place the fish in it. Bring slowly to the boil and cook very gently for 8 to 10 minutes. The surface of the liquid should hardly break. Remove the container from the heat and, when cool enough to handle, remove the fish from the cooking liquid and carefully unwrap them, one by one. The two fillets should be lifted from each fish and placed either in individual shallow dishes or soup plates or in a single layer in one large dish.

All the skin and bones should be returned to the *court bouillon*, together with the spices and bay leaves, but not the lavender, and the whole should be simmered very gently for 20 minutes. Carefully strain into a

serves 6

one 75 cl bottle dry white wine
1 litre / 36 fl oz water
150 ml / 5 fl oz white wine vinegar
   or lavender vinegar (p.34)
6 medium rainbow trout
1 tablespoon sea salt
$\frac{1}{2}$ teaspoon black peppercorns,
   coarsely crushed
$\frac{1}{2}$ teaspoon white peppercorns,
   coarsely crushed
$\frac{1}{2}$ teaspoon allspice (Jamaica
   pepper), coarsely crushed
3 cloves
a generous splinter of cinnamon
about 0.5 cm / $\frac{1}{4}$ inch fresh
   ginger
3 bay leaves
a pinch of saffron
2 or 3 lavender spikes, plus extra
   for decoration, together with
   some glossy greenery such as
   purslane or watercress

saucepan, return to the boil and simmer to reduce the liquid by two-thirds. Add the lavender spikes and then remove the stock from the heat. Allow to cool for 20–30 minutes, which will also give time for the lavender to infuse, then pour it gently over the fish, reserving about 50 ml/2 fl oz. Place somewhere cool, then refrigerate and, when the jelly begins to set, use the liquid you have set aside to paint on the surface of the fish to give it a nice glossy coat.

This somewhat elaborate recipe is best made in the morning for an afternoon or evening meal, rather than the day before and then refrigerated – too much time in the fridge will mute the sparkling fresh flavours.

Lavender-smoked salmon fillets

I learned how to smoke food in Bruce Cost's kitchen in San Francisco, where he showed me how to make tea-smoked duck and salmon in a wok. Since then I have used his method for many recipes, scenting the smoke with dried fennel twigs, different varieties of tea, oak chips, dried orange peel and lavender stalks and flowers. This last works very well with salmon and duck, both of which are rich enough to match the haunting fragrance.

Put the salmon in a shallow dish and cover with the brine. Leave for 30 minutes, then remove, rinse and dry the fish fillets. Toast the salt and peppers lightly in a wok and – when cool – crush them and rub them all over the salmon.

Line a wok with a double thickness of foil and put the rice, sugar and lavender in the bottom of the wok. Place the rack on top, grease it lightly and arrange the salmon fillets on it. Put the lid on and seal the edge with foil or rolled up, damp paper towels.

Place the wok on medium-high heat and, once the rice and sugar have begun to smoke – which you will smell rather than see – resist the temptation to open

serves 6

six 150 g/5 oz salmon fillets
300 ml/½ pint brine made with
   30 g/1 oz salt and
   300 ml/½ pint water
1 tablespoon coarse sea salt
1 tablespoon Sechuan pepper
½ tablespoon black peppercorns
100 g/4 oz *uncooked* rice
100 g/4 oz sugar
a handful of lavender stalks and a
   few flowers

Lavender-smoked salmon fillets /continued

the lid and leave it for 15 to 20 minutes. Remove
from the heat and, with the lid still on, leave for a
further 15 minutes. Serve the fish warm or cold, with
a lemon butter sauce or mayonnaise flavoured with
lavender vinegar (p.34).

Cook's tip

A wok with a glass rather than a metal lid makes the perfect home
smoker.

Goat's cheese, fig and lavender ramekins

You will need to begin preparing this summery first
course at least a day before you eat it.

Put the lavender flowers in a bowl, bring the oil to the
boil, pour it over the lavender and leave to infuse for a
day or even two.

Line six ramekins with cling film. Put the goat's cheese
in a bowl, season it lightly and then mix it with a fork
until you have a homogeneous mass. Spoon half the
cheese into the ramekins to a depth of about 1 cm/
½ inch, pressing it down. Spread the dried figs on top,
then divide the rest of the goat's cheese and spoon it
over the figs. Press down well, smoothing the surface.
Cover with cling film and refrigerate for a couple of
hours.

Carefully turn out and serve on a bed of small salad
leaves. Arrange slices of fresh fig on top and spoon the
lavender-infused olive oil around and on top of the
cheese. Splash on a little white wine or lavender
vinegar (p.34) and arrange the sprigs of lavender on
top of the cheeses.

serves 6

1 or 2 teaspoons fresh lavender
    flowers
150 ml/5 fl oz mild and fruity
    olive oil
300 g/12 oz fresh goat's cheese
6 dried figs, chopped small
2 fresh figs
salt
pepper

Garnish
violet or green olives, depending
    on the colour of the fresh figs
6 sprigs lavender

Roast duck with lavender honey and sesame seeds

When I first cooked at the Mandarin Oriental Hotel in Hong Kong, I ate many magnificent dishes prepared by the chef Jurg Muensch. One of them was pigeon caramelised with lavender honey. I adapted the recipe to duck, which takes very well to this fragrant herb.

First, make the 'lavender honey'. You can, of course, buy lavender honey, which is a mono-floral honey produced by bees that have fed only on the nectar of lavender flowers. Spain, France, Italy and Croatia all produce excellent lavender honey, but it can be difficult to come by and anyway it does not always have a distinctive lavender scent or flavour.

To make your own lavender honey, simply empty the contents of a jar or two of neutral clear honey into a saucepan and add 6-8 lavender sprigs. Heat almost to boiling, remove from the heat and infuse the honey until it is cold. Remove the lavender and re-pot the honey. You can add a sprig of lavender to each jar for further flavour.

Prick the duck's skin all over and rub it with the juice of half a lime. Squeeze the juice from the other half of the lime and reserve it. Put the lime skins inside the duck cavity, rub the bird all over with soy sauce, paint it with lavender honey and set it on its breast on a trivet in a roasting tin.

Roast for 30 minutes at 200°C/400°F/gas mark 6. Remove briefly from the oven and carefully drain off the fat and any juices. Put the duck back on the rack breast side upwards, brush it with a little more soy sauce and honey and roast for a further 20 minutes.

Again briefly remove from the oven, drain off the fat and juices, scatter on the sesame seeds and finish roasting for another 10 to 15 minutes. When the duck is cooked, juices should run clear when you pierce the thigh.

Remove the bird from the oven, cover loosely with

serves 4

a duckling weighing about
2 kg / 4 lb
1 lime, cut in half
2 tablespoons soy sauce
2–3 tablespoons lavender honey, melted to liquid
2 tablespoons sesame seeds
2 tablespoons toasted sesame oil
1 tablespoon lime juice or rice vinegar

Roast duck with lavender honey /continued

foil and let it rest for 15 minutes or so while you decide what to do with the fat and juices. Ideally, these should be separated, and you can then boil up the juices with any remaining honey and the reserved lime juice, adding the toasted sesame oil when you take it off the boil. Use this as a piquant oriental dressing or gravy for the duck. I serve this with rice and steamed or stir-fried oriental greens. The duck is also very good served cold with a noodle salad.

Duck breasts with a honey, lavender and cider glaze

This is another version of duck with lavender and honey flavours; it is based on a dish I devised for a series of dinners I cooked at the Café Royal. It is a good recipe for large numbers, as neat duck breasts are more manageable than whole birds. If you want to cook twice the number, simply add another roasting tray.

Score the fat on the duck breasts in small lozenges. Remove the arrow-shaped fillets loosely attached to the underside of the duck breasts and use them for another dish. Bring the cider, honey, lavender, Calvados and vinegar to the boil. Allow to cool, then brush on the duck skin and place it, skin side downwards, in a shallow dish. Leave overnight.

Cook the onions in the duck stock until soft, then sieve, season with salt, pepper and nutmeg, and whisk in the cream. Put the sauce to one side. Cook the duck in a heavy frying pan or a very hot oven – 220°C/420°F/gas mark 7 – for approximately two-thirds of the time on the skin side and one-third on the other, to give a well-coloured crisp skin.

Drain off all the fat before serving the meat with the onion sauce. When serving this dish at the Café Royal, we also minced the duck fillet, mixed it with herbs and breadcrumbs and used this forcemeat to

serves 8

8 duck breasts
100 ml/4 fl oz dry cider
75 ml/3 fl oz lavender honey
(p.111)
4 sprigs lavender
2 tablespoons Calvados
1 tablespoon cider vinegar
500 g/1 lb onions, sliced
300 ml/1/2 pint duck stock
a good pinch of nutmeg
2–3 tablespoons double cream
salt
pepper
extra lavender and other herbs for garnish

stuff cabbage leaves rolled into balls. In summer, when you will be using fresh lavender, you could stuff fresh vine leaves, chard or spinach.

Roast stuffed shoulder of lamb with lavender and caper sauce

Using the inexpensive shoulder, which lends itself perfectly to slow, easy roasting, this recipe is ideal for a late Sunday lunch. I love this method of cooking lamb, which results in sweet, tender meat, almost falling from the bone. Capers and lavender flowers enhance the Mediterranean flavours of this dish.

Ask your butcher to remove the two large bones from a shoulder of lamb, but to leave in the knuckle bone. This makes for much easier carving. Remove as much visible fat as possible.

Pre-heat the oven to 230°C/450°F/gas mark 8. Mix all the stuffing ingredients together and place in the centre of the opened-out shoulder. Fold over the edges of the meat, tie it round three times to form a rosette shape and place in a roasting tin.

Roast for 20 minutes, then turn the heat down to 150°C/300°F/gas mark 3 and roast slowly for about 2 to 2½ hours. Allow the meat to rest for at least 15 minutes in a warm place before carving.

At the same time as you put the lamb in the oven, you can add a dish of potatoes and onions. Peel and thinly slice both, then layer them in an oiled oven-proof dish, lightly seasoning each layer with a little salt and pepper and a trickle of olive oil. This is even better if you place the lamb on top of the vegetables for the last hour of cooking, together with any juices from which you have skimmed off the fat.

Stir the flour into the oil in a saucepan on a low heat and cook for 5 minutes to make a roux. Gradually blend in the stock and cook for 5 minutes or so, until

serves 4 to 6

a shoulder of lamb, boned as described, weighing about 1.5 kg/3 lb (boned weight)

For the stuffing
100 g/4 oz fresh soft breadcrumbs
2 tablespoons extra virgin olive oil
1 small onion, chopped
2 tablespoons toasted pine kernels
2 tablespoons sultanas or chopped dried apricots
2–3 cloves garlic, crushed
grated rind and juice of 1 lemon
grated rind and juice of 1 orange
1 tablespoon finely chopped chervil, basil or parsley
½ teaspoon thyme
½ teaspoon lavender flowers

Caper and lavender sauce
1 tablespoon olive oil
1 tablespoon flour
300 ml/½ pint lamb stock
2–3 tablespoons capers (well-rinsed, if salted)
½ teaspoon lavender flowers
zest and juice of ½ lemon
salt
pepper

Roast stuffed shoulder of lamb /continued

the sauce is smooth and the flour no longer tastes raw.
Stir in the capers, lavender, lemon zest and juice, bring
to the boil and season with salt and pepper.

Cook's tip

In winter, when fresh lavender is not available, I use Seville orange
zest and juice in place of the lemon and rosemary instead of
lavender. The caper and lavender combination also goes well with
mutton or kid.

Fragrant lamb tagine

Inspired by thoughts of lavender couscous, I have
included lavender to good effect in my standard recipe
for lamb tagine.

Trim any excess fat from the lamb and cut the meat
into 5 cm/2 inch cubes. Brown them in the olive oil
and put to one side. Lightly brown the onion and
then add the garlic and spices, including the lavender.
Cook these dry for 2 to 3 minutes and then gradually
add the stock, scraping up the residues.

Put the meat in a casserole, pour the spiced stock and
onion over it and add the carrots, apricots and lemon
to the pot. Cover and cook at 180°C/350°F/gas mark
4 for 1 to 1 1/2 hours. Simmer for about 15 to 20
minutes before the end and, just before serving, grind
on some nutmeg and scatter with the chopped
coriander leaves and a few sprigs of lavender.

serves 4 to 6

750 g/1 1/2 lb lamb, off the bone
1 tablespoon olive oil
1 medium onion, chopped
2–3 cloves garlic, crushed
1/2 teaspoon ground cinnamon
1/2 teaspoon ground cardamom
1 teaspoon cumin seeds
1 teaspoon coriander seeds,
    crushed
1 teaspoon lavender flowers
200 ml/7 fl oz lamb stock
4 carrots or small turnips, coarsely
    sliced
150 g/5 oz dried apricots, soaked
    in warm water for 1/2 hour
1/2 preserved lemon, or juice and
    pared zest of 1/2 lemon
salt and pepper

For decoration
nutmeg
fresh coriander leaves
half a dozen sprigs of lavender

Rabbit with lavender

I developed this recipe when writing a series on cooking methods for the much-missed magazine *A la carte*. Rabbit's meat is very delicate, and steaming is an excellent way of cooking it.

Carefully remove the two fillets and flaps from each side of the backbone, scraping down from the spine and over the ribs with a sharp knife; you can use the legs in a rabbit and mustard casserole. Place the two fillets from each saddle side by side, with the flaps overlapping, leaving a 'channel' to stuff. Slide 7 or 8 lengths of string under the meat, so that you will be able to tie the stuffed roll at intervals.

Mix the breadcrumbs, cheese, lemon zest, parsley, lavender and a little seasoning. If the mixture seems very dry, moisten it with white wine or mix in some lightly beaten egg, but not too much. Spoon this into the 'channel', lightly pressing it to fill the space. Carefully bring the edges together and tie the stuffed fillets, pushing back any stuffing that escapes. Stuff the other two fillets in the same way.

Using a steamer, put 600 ml/1 pint water in the base together with the 6 lavender sprigs. Cover, bring to the boil, remove from the heat and allow to infuse for 10 minutes. Put the rabbit on the steamer rack, cover with a tight-fitting lid and bring the water slowly back to the boil. Steam the rabbit for about 35 minutes over simmering water. Remove from the heat and allow to rest before carving into slices and serving. The bones and trimmings can be used in advance to make a stock, and then a sauce while the rabbit is steaming. I like to serve this with wilted spinach and wild or brown rice, with some lavender heads for garnish.

serves 4

2 saddles of rabbit
200 g / 7 oz soft white
    breadcrumbs
100 g / 4 oz Cheddar or
    Parmesan, grated
finely pared zest of 1 lemon
2 tablespoons flat leaf parsley,
    finely chopped
1 or 2 teaspoons lavender flowers
6 sprigs lavender, plus extra for
    garnish
salt
pepper

Lavender and cider baked ham

This is a lovely dish for a summer lunch, a feast for carnivorous friends.

Mix the glaze ingredients first. The quantities given here are guidelines only, to give an idea of the proportions. Rub some of the glaze on the ham before cooking it.

Wrap the ham in a triple thickness of buttered foil, on a bed of quartered onions and with a few lavender stalks tucked around it. Place in a roasting tin and bake for 4 hours in an oven pre-heated to 150°C/300°F/ gas mark 3. Then turn the heat up to 190°C/375°F/ gas mark 5 for 1 hour. Alternatively, allow about 40-45 minutes per kilo at 180°C/350°F/gas mark 4. The ham is cooked when the 'mustard spoon' bone wiggles quite freely.

There will be plenty of liquid in the foil parcel, and this, when carefully poured off, together with the soft onions, can be rubbed through a sieve to provide one of the accompaniments, a subtle, unusual and well-flavoured sauce to which you can add cream if you wish.

When cool enough to handle, remove the skin, keeping only a thin layer of fat. Score this in lozenges, brush or rub the glaze all over and stick cloves and lavender flowers in a decorative pattern over the ham's surface. Bake in the oven at 220°C/425°F/gas mark 7 for 20 minutes and then let it stand for 10 to 15 minutes before carving. Fresh lavender can be used to decorate if you wish. New potatoes, either freshly boiled or in a salad, are the perfect accompaniment, as is a salad of peas, beans and Little Gem lettuce. Or you may prefer a pasta salad or spicy rice.

serves 12 with generous leftovers

a whole uncooked ham on the
  bone, 4–5 kg/8–10 lb
several stalks of lavender, in bud
  or flower
500 g/1 lb onions, quartered

Glaze
3 tablespoons lavender honey
  (p.111)
2 tablespoons lavender vinegar
  (p.34)
1 tablespoon English grain
  mustard
1 teaspoon freshly ground black
  pepper

Garnish
30 cloves and 12 lavender flowers

Leg of kid *boulangère*

This is another recipe based on my cooking in the West Country, where I was able to buy excellent kid. There was a lavender bush growing at the farmhouse door, so the two seemed made for each other. Kid is a really excellent meat – lean, tender and full of flavour.

Brown the joint all over in 1 to 2 tablespoons of the olive oil. Peel the garlic, cut it into thin slivers and insert them under the thin layer of fat and skin.

Pre-heat the oven to 180°C/350°F/gas mark 4. Put half the potatoes and onions in the bottom of a well-soaked chicken brick or a roasting tin, lay the meat on top and cover with the rest of the onions. Add the herbs, season lightly and pour on the wine and the rest of the olive oil. Put on the lid and cook for about 2 ½ hours, or until the meat is tender. Timing will depend on the age, and therefore the tenderness, of the animal.

Serve crowned with lavender and parsley.

serves 4

a leg of goat weighing about 1.5 kg/3 lb
4 tablespoons olive oil
1 head of garlic
2 large onions, thinly sliced
3 or 4 potatoes, thinly sliced
half a dozen sprigs of lavender
a few sprigs of parsley
1 glass of dry white or red wine
salt
pepper

Garnish
lavender and parsley

Tomato and lavender tart

Here I pair tomato with lavender as a change from basil or mint, its more usual partners. It makes an exquisite vegetarian first course for a summer meal. The base is bread dough rather than short pastry.

Sift the dry ingredients together and then stir in the water. You may not require all the water, or you may need a little more, to produce a soft – but not sticky – dough. Knead for 10 minutes on a floured work-top until you have a smooth, elastic dough. Put the dough in an oiled bowl, cover with a damp cloth and leave it to rise.

When the dough has doubled in volume, knock it back and knead it lightly once more. Working on a floured work surface, roll and stretch it to fit an oiled

serves 4

300 g/10 oz strong plain flour
1 teaspoon fast action yeast
1 teaspoon salt
150–200 ml/5–7 fl oz water
2 tablespoons olive oil (optional)
50 ml/2 fl oz extra virgin olive oil
6 cloves garlic, thinly sliced (optional)
750 g/1 ½ lb firm, ripe tomatoes, sliced
1 teaspoon chopped lavender flowers
salt
pepper

Tomato and lavender tart /continued

shallow tart tin about 25–30 cm/10–12 inches in diameter, pressing the dough up the sides to form a wall. Brush the dough all over with olive oil, and, if using it, scatter slices of garlic on the bottom.

Arrange the tomato slices in overlapping circles and brush with the remaining oil. Sprinkle on the lavender flowers and lightly season with salt and pepper, cover and let the dough prove once again for about 45 minutes. Bake for 20 to 25 minutes in the top half of an oven pre-heated to 200°C/400°F/gas mark 6.

This tart is best eaten warm, or at room temperature, but should not be refrigerated.

Pilaff of wild rice with lavender and toasted almonds

I find the volume method of measuring most useful for this recipe, using a measuring jug.

Put the rice in a saucepan with the water, bring to the boil, stir, cover and then cook on the lowest possible heat until the water has been absorbed and the rice grains are broken open and cooked as you like, either chewy or soft. This can take from 25 to 50 minutes.

Heat the oil in a frying pan and fry the shallots until soft, then stir in the almonds and fry until these are golden. Add the flowers and the rice, stir well to coat with the oil and heat through until the rice is hot and the flowers have released their fragrance. Serve at once with roast chicken or guinea fowl, or griddled pheasant breasts. This scented rice also makes an excellent stuffing for poultry, especially quail.

serves 4

125 ml/4.5 fl oz wild rice
375 ml/12 fl oz water or
    vegetable or chicken stock
2 tablespoons extra virgin olive oil
    or butter
2 shallots, finely chopped
2 or 3 tablespoons flaked almonds
1 or two teaspoons lavender
    flowers
wild rice cooked as above

Cook's tip

You can vary the texture of this pilaff by using toasted hazelnuts, pecans or walnuts.

Lavender shallot vinegar

I once used lavender vinegar (p.34) with shallots by accident when serving with oysters. It was delicious! What I do now, however, is to mix half lavender vinegar and half red wine vinegar with the finely chopped fresh shallots, as the latter gives a delicate lavender tint to the condiment.

Lavender mayonnaise

You need only a teaspoon or two of well-infused lavender vinegar (p.34) to flavour quite a large batch of mayonnaise, say 300 ml/10 fl oz.

Herb and flower salad with walnut oil and lavender vinaigrette

Crush a handful of shelled walnuts quite small, add a good pinch of sea salt and a small pinch of English mustard, freshly ground black pepper and two tablespoons lavender vinegar (p.34). Whisk in 6 to 8 tablespoons of walnut oil and you have your vinaigrette.

For your salad bowl, use small lettuce and spinach leaves, tender sorrel, rocket, watercress, chervil, basil, flat-leaf parsley, purslane, salad burnet, tender nasturtium leaves and any other greens you feel suitable. Carefully turn in the vinaigrette and garnish the salad with edible flowers.

Marigolds and nasturtiums

Marigolds and nasturtiums are essential summer ingredients in my kitchen, not so much for their fragrance as for their lively peppery flavour, glorious colour and, in the case of nasturtiums, their splendidly baroque shape.

'... and winking Marybuds begin to open their golden eyes.'

William Shakespeare, *Cymbeline*

Marigolds

The marigold in question is the pot marigold, *Calendula officinalis*, not French, African or Mexican marigolds, which are different flowers altogether. The pot marigold is a native European plant with several English names, including Holigold and Mary Gold, which, with Marybud, is explained by the medieval legend that the Virgin Mary wore golden blossoms, which led the monks to name the flower in her honour. Poets began calling the flower 'Mary Gowles' and 'Mary Golde', and so it was that Marybuds found their way into Shakespeare's *Cymbeline*.

This simple garden flower has numerous medicinal applications and it is still used today in herbal and homoeopathic medicine. Infusions and lotions made from its petals are said to benefit the complexion, and the flowers provide an instant antidote to insect stings.

Marigold has long been employed in the kitchen, especially as a colouring. The petals contain carotene and lycopene and have often been used as an inexpensive substitute for saffron and also to colour cheese and butter. The petals give a subtle, spicy flavour and golden tint to seafood dishes, soups, fish stews, milk puddings, risottos and egg dishes.

Dorothy Hartley quotes a 'very old' recipe in which thinly sliced apples are baked in the bottom of a pie crust, eggs are then beaten with milk, salt, pepper, thyme, a little sage and a lot of marigold petals, the custard poured over the apples and baked. It was said to have been served with roast pork, rather as Yorkshire pudding accompanies roast beef.

You can also add the petals to cakes, breads, scones and biscuits. They can be crystallised in the usual way (see p.36), but I have also come across a description of the flower heads being carefully divided into three or four and the whole section being frosted or crystallised, which gives a very pleasing fan shape.

It is worth drying marigold petals if you like the colour and flavour they impart to food (see p.48). Infused in a little boiling water or milk, they can be added to a risotto, a pancake batter or what you will.

Terrine of goat's cheese with marigold potatoes and leeks

This terrine makes a stunning first course to a vegetarian meal, although I have yet to meet a carnivore who does not enjoy it, and I often serve it as a first course for non-vegetarians. It also looks splendid as part of a summer buffet.

I used to make this with whole baby leeks, but find that it slices more easily without long 'strings' of leeks. If you're not partial to goat's milk and its by-products, you can use another soft cheese.

Boil the potatoes until just tender, drain and slice

serves 10

4 or 5 large waxy potatoes
6 large leeks, sliced
500 g / 1 lb soft goat's cheese
2 handfuls of marigold petals
salt
pepper

Terrine of goat's cheese /continued

them thinly when cool enough to handle. Remove the outer leaves from the leeks and boil them until soft but still bright green. Take half the goat's cheese and mix in the marigold petals with a fork.

Oil a terrine and layer the potatoes with the leeks and goat's cheese – both plain and that mixed with the marigold petals – finishing with a layer of potatoes, seasoning each layer lightly. Cover the terrine with food wrap and weight it down very heavily for at least 4 hours, or overnight, to make for easier slicing.

This goes very well with a lentil and walnut salad, dressed with walnut rather than olive oil, and with a few marigold petals to decorate the plate.

Cheddar and marigold scones

These scones can be served warm as an accompaniment to a thick soup for a satisfying lunch or supper. They are very good at breakfast-time with scrambled eggs, and can also be used as a base for a version of eggs Benedict.

Rub the flour, butter and cheese together with your finger-tips until the mixture resembles coarse breadcrumbs. Add the petals and stir in enough liquid to make a soft, pliable dough. Transfer to a floured work-top and knead lightly and briefly until smooth.

Roll out the dough to a thickness of about 3 cm/generous 1 inch and cut out the scones. Bake in an oven pre-heated to 200°C/400°F/gas mark 6 for about 15 to 18 minutes, until the scones are well-risen and golden.

makes 10 to 12

300 g/10 oz self-raising flour sifted with ½ teaspoon hot paprika
50g/2 oz butter, chilled and diced
50 g/2 oz grated Cheddar
4 tablespoons marigold petals
150–175 ml/5–6 fl oz soured milk or buttermilk

Cook's tip

My mother taught me to put scones close together on the baking sheet to encourage them to rise well and evenly. It never fails, and gives a nice tender edge to the scone.

For sweet scones, leave out the cheese and paprika and replace them with 3 or 4 tablespoons of sultanas or chopped mixed peel and 50 g/2 oz of golden caster sugar.

Marigold and orange sponge

This is a classic Victoria sponge recipe, perfect for a summer tea. You can also serve it freshly baked and still warm as a pudding, in which case I would leave out the butter cream and serve a single wedge of the cake per serving, dusted with icing sugar and with a scoop of clotted cream on the side.

Grind the sugar and marigold petals in a food-processor, then cream the butter and sugar thoroughly until it is pale, light and fluffy. Add the zest and juice, and then the eggs, gradually folding them into the creamed mixture. Once the eggs have been incorporated, gently fold in the flour.

Spoon the batter into two 20 cm / 8 inch greased and floured sandwich tins, smooth the top and bake for 20 to 25 minutes in an oven pre-heated to 180°C/350°F/gas mark 4.

Allow to cool in the tin for a few minutes, then ease out the sponges and allow them to cool on wire racks. To serve, sandwich with a marigold butter cream and sift icing sugar over the top.

serves 8 to 10

175 g/6 oz golden granulated
   sugar
2 handfuls of marigold petals
175 g/6 oz unsalted butter, at
   room temperature
finely pared zest and juice of
   1 orange
4 medium-size eggs, lightly beaten
175 g/6 oz self-raising flour, sifted

Marigold and orange butter cream

Mix the ingredients together thoroughly and, while it is still soft, spread the butter cream on one half of the sponge.

makes enough for one cake

75 g/3 oz unsalted butter,
   softened
50 g/2 oz unrefined icing sugar
1 handful of marigold petals
   crushed with 1 tablespoon
   caster sugar
pared zest of 1 orange
1–2 tablespoons orange juice

Marigold muffins

As long as they are not too sweet, muffins of all kinds are good for breakfast, not least because they are quick and easy to make.

Mix the dry ingredients, including the petals, then stir in the wet ingredients until just combined. The mixture should remain somewhat lumpy and not be over-mixed. Spoon into double paper cases set on a baking sheet and bake in an oven pre-heated to 180°C/350°F/gas mark 4 for 15 to 20 minutes, until well-risen and golden brown.

makes 6 large or 12 smaller muffins

175 g/6 oz plain flour
1 tablespoon baking powder
50 g/2 oz sugar
3 tablespoons marigold petals
75 g/3 oz butter, melted
2 eggs, lightly beaten

Cook's tip

2 tablespoons of ground almonds can be substituted for 25 g/1 oz of flour. For fruit and nut muffins, add 2 tablespoons of raisins or other dried fruit (chopped if necessary) and 2 tablespoons of chopped nuts.

Nasturtiums

Nasturtium, or *Tropaeolum majus* was brought to Spain in the sixteenth century by the conquistadores, who had seen the Amerindians using it to treat respiratory ailments and as an antibacterial. English herbals of the time refer to the plant as Indian cress. Nasturtium means 'nose-twister' in Latin, a reference, perhaps, to the expression on one's face after eating a particularly peppery specimen. And quite strong flavours do indeed develop in the flower, the leaves and the seeds, especially under a hot sun. Indeed, in times of shortage the dried and ground seeds have been used as a pepper substitute.

Thanks to seedsmen, yellow, orange and vermilion flowers are now joined by even more subtle shades of peach, tangerine and cherry red, but they all taste the same — spicy, peppery and with a hint of sweetness. Because they are not used for their fragrance, nasturtiums need no advance preparation, such as infusing or making into flavoured sugar; I simply use the flower directly in the dish it is to flavour or colour. Egg dishes, mayonnaise and hollandaise, rice and pasta dishes, cream cheese, pancake batter and pale cream vegetable soups all benefit from a hot burst of colour and flavour. And salads also warm to these lovely flowers, especially the dark green of spinach and the pale green of romaine lettuce. Try them too on a platter of cool cucumber salad. It is in connection with nasturtiums that Mrs Beeton makes one of her very few comments about the use of flowers in the kitchen: 'Many consider them a good adjunct to salads, to which they certainly add a pretty appearance.'

'The seeds of this rare and faire plant came from the Indies into Spaine, and thence into France and Flanders, from whence I received seed that bore with me both floures & seed, especially those I received from my loving friend John Robin of Paris.'

John Gerard

Historie of Plants, 1633

Something over a hundred years earlier, we find
Hannah Glasse using nasturtiums. She gives two
recipes for salmagundy, or 'salamongundy', an
elaborate composed salad involving nasturtiums,
called 'stertion flowers' in one recipe, 'station flowers'
in another, to decorate the dish. In both cases, the
dishes have a contemporary ring to them, combining
chicken, romaine lettuce, hard-boiled eggs, cresses,
nasturtiums and anchovies, all sliced, diced and
arranged as attractively as possible. Miss Glasse also
refers to 'astertion buds' – her spelling was highly
individual, phonetic in many cases (her 'giam' for 'jam'
is another example). It is little surprise that, over the
years, recipes got changed in transcription and
re-transcription by generations of cooks.

If you have patience and a steady hand, you can stuff
nasturtium flowers, which are surprisingly robust.
Softened cream cheese mixed with chives, or chervil,
curried egg salad, spiced rice or chicken mousse all
work well, although the stuffing must be very fine in
order to pipe or spoon it into the tiny throat of the
flower. Serve each stuffed flower on a nasturtium leaf.

Nasturtium leaves, buds and seeds also have their place
in the kitchen. The buds and seeds can be pickled and
used as you would capers, although you sacrifice the
flowers if you use the buds. Be patient and use any
seeds that are left. Of course, if you have eaten all the
flowers, you won't have any seeds. Whole small leaves
and chopped larger leaves make a delightfully peppery
addition to a green salad.

Even if you only have space for a window box, a
hanging basket or a tub, a few nasturtium seeds are well
worth planting, as they grow and spread throughout
the summer if they are in a sunny spot.

Nasturtium salad

This recipe turns up in many books, including Florence White's *Flowers as Food*, a collection of flower recipes and lore accumulated by the author over many years. She also gives an almost identical recipe taken from a *Housewife's Notebook* of 1922. In each case the accompanying herb is chervil and the only other ingredients are salt, lemon juice and olive oil.

It may have originated in Turabi Effendi's *Turkish Cookery Book* of 1864, for it is quoted as such in *Aromas and Flavours of Past and Present*, by Alice B. Toklas, annotated by the irritating Poppy Cannon. The recipe is as simple and pleasing now as it was when it was first invented, whenever that was.

'Put a plate of the flowers of nasturtium in a bowl, with a tablespoon of chopped chervil. Sprinkle over with your fingers ½ teaspoon salt, pour over 2 or 3 tablespoons olive oil and the juice of a lemon. Turn the salad in the bowl with a spoon and fork until well mixed and serve.'

Nasturtium and pumpkin seed bread

The pumpkin seeds add a chewy texture and the flowers a burst of colour to this easy and versatile bread recipe.

Mix the dry ingredients in a bowl, make a well in the centre and pour in the oil and water. Draw the flour into the centre and mix well, until the dough leaves the sides of the bowl. Once the flour and liquid are combined, quickly work in the seeds and petals. Alternatively, you can make the dough in a food-processor.

Turn the dough onto a floured surface and knead it for five minutes. Shape the dough and put it into a lightly greased 1 kg / 2 lb loaf tin. Cover loosely with lightly oiled cling film and let it rise in a moderately warm place for about an hour, by when it should have doubled in size.

Bake for about 35 to 40 minutes in an oven pre-heated to 200°C/400°F/gas mark 6. Turn the loaf onto a wire rack and cool completely before slicing.

makes a 1 kg/2 lb loaf

500 g / 1 lb strong white flour
2 teaspoons salt
2 teaspoons fast-action
 dried yeast
2 tablespoons olive oil
generous 300 ml / ½ pint
 warm water
75 g / 3 oz pumpkin seeds
10 nasturtium flowers, shredded
1 tablespoon fresh nasturtium
 seeds, chopped

Cook's tip

In devising your own recipes based on this bread mixture, remember the following proportions:

1 teaspoon salt to approx 250 g / 8 oz flour
approximately half liquid to flour

500 g / 1 lb flour will make 12 to 18 bread rolls; these will bake at the same temperature in about 15 minutes

Try mixing wholemeal and white flour for a different loaf and experimenting with additions of other grains and seeds, such as sunflower and sesame. If you make an entirely wholemeal loaf, you will find you need to add a little more water. Marigold petals and fennel flowers are also good in bread, and you might want to add a little grated cheese for a savoury loaf.

Peppery golden hotcakes

I like to make hotcakes for late, lazy breakfasts. Sometimes I put fruit such as blueberries in them, but in the summer I like to use nasturtium or marigold petals, or a mixture of golden flowers. You will need very little oil or butter if you use a non-stick pan to cook these hotcakes.

Beat the egg, milk, yoghurt and flour to make a thick, smooth, lump-free batter. Stir in the baking powder and the flowers, then wait until the batter begins to froth and bubble slightly on the surface. This indicates that the mixture is aerating because of the baking powder's action and will produce a light batter.

Make sure the pan and the fat are hot. Pour in the batter until it covers the area of a small saucer. Do not shake the pan or spread the mixture. When the surface is matt, dry and full of holes, turn it over and cook the underside for 2 to 3 minutes. Stack the hotcakes on a plate set over a pan of hot water until you have used all the batter.

Maple syrup and whipped butter are the classic accompaniments, but try them with a Fennel Flower and Lemon Syrup (p.73) or a flower butter (p.24) for a sublime breakfast.

makes 6 to 7 large cakes

1 egg
150 ml / 5 fl oz semi-skimmed or
    skimmed milk
1 heaped tablespoon plain yoghurt
125 g / 4 oz plain flour
1 teaspoon baking powder
3 tablespoons chopped marigold
    and nasturtium petals
sunflower oil or butter for frying

Cod in saffron broth with nasturtium mayonnaise

This is a bright and lively dish for early summer. It is important that the cod fillets be evenly-sized. Salmon is also very tasty when combined with the same flavours.

Lightly season the fish and put it to one side. Heat the oil in a large saucepan or casserole and gently cook the shallots and garlic for 5 to 10 minutes, without browning them.

Add the turnips and potatoes, turn them in the oil and then add the saffron and the liquid. Bring to the boil and simmer until the vegetables are barely tender. Place the cod fillets on top of the vegetables, partially cover and let the water barely simmer for 5 to 10 minutes, depending on the thickness of the cod and how well-done you like your fish.

Carefully transfer the fish to large shallow bowls, spoon the vegetables around it, adding a little of the broth. Garnish with a nasturtium leaf, a couple of flowers and a sprig of chervil and serve with nasturtium mayonnaise.

serves 4

4 x 150−200 g/6−7 oz cod
 fillets, skinned
2−3 tablespoons extra virgin
 olive oil
salt
pepper
2 shallots, thinly sliced
2 cloves garlic, thinly sliced
4 small turnips, cut into wedges
500 g/1 lb potatoes, cut into
 wedges
a good pinch of saffron
1 litre/2 pints fish stock or white
 wine and water mixed

To serve
chervil
nasturtium flowers and leaves

Nasturtium mayonnaise

Put the flowers in a mortar and grind with the salt, then stir into a bowl of home-made mayonnaise, which can be as garlicky as you like. You can also shred some small tender nasturtium leaves and stir them into the mayonnaise.

5 or 6 nasturtium flowers
1/2 teaspoon coarse sea salt
250 ml/8 fl oz home-made
 mayonnaise

Cook's tip

Marigolds, fennel flowers and other herb flowers can be used in similar fashion to make flavoured mayonnaises.

Chicken quilted with nasturtiums and chives

The stuffing goes under the chicken's skin, which keeps the bird beautifully moist. Chive flowers make an attractive garnish for this distinctively flavoured dish.

Remove any visible fat from the bird's cavity and ease the skin away from its flesh by gradually inserting your fingers between the skin and the breasts. Continue working your way round the bird until the skin is loose around the legs and back. Mix together the nasturtiums, chives and cream cheese and spread the mixture over the flesh, under the skin, then ease the skin back into place. This is all much easier than it sounds.

Season the chicken inside and out. Prick the lemon all over with a skewer and put it in the cavity. Cover the bird loosely, but carefully, with foil and roast it in a pre-heated oven at 200°C/400°F/gas mark 6 for about 1½ hours. Allow the chicken to rest for 10 to 15 minutes, then serve on a platter surrounded with nasturtium and chive flowers. Rice cooked in the oven with some chopped flowers in it is an excellent accompaniment, together with a crisp green salad.

serves 4

a chicken weighing 1.5 kg/3 lb
6 nasturtium flowers, torn into
    pieces, plus extra flowers to
    garnish
25 g/1 oz chives
250 g/8 oz cream cheese
1 lemon
sea salt
black pepper

Carrot, celery and nasturtium risotto

One of the nicest risottos I have ever eaten was in Florence, and it couldn't have been simpler – no expensive foie gras, truffles or porcini, just finely diced carrots and celery. I have taken it one step further with the addition of golden nasturtium flowers, which somehow enhance the rusticity of the dish. A deep, heavy frying pan is needed for cooking risotto.

Chop and fry the shallots – without browning them – for 4 to 5 minutes in the olive oil. Then stir in the rice until it is well coated with the oil.

Bring the wine and the stock to the boil in separate pans. Pour a couple of ladles of wine over the rice, stir well and, when it has been absorbed by the rice, add the rest of the wine. When this too has been absorbed, add the stock, a little at a time, allowing the rice to absorb it before adding more. Add the chopped carrots with the first batch of stock and then, after 5 minutes or so, add the celery. Stir the risotto from time to time.

The rice may be cooked to your liking before you have used up all the stock. I like risotto quite soft, moist and creamy, rather than dry. Just before serving, tear up the first batch of nasturtium flowers and stir into the risotto. To serve, place a nasturtium flower on each serving and pass around the Parmesan cheese and a grater.

serves 4 to 6

2 shallots
2 tablespoons extra virgin olive oil
350 g / 12 oz arborio or
    vialone rice
300 ml / ½ pint dry white wine
1 litre / 2 pints chicken or
    vegetable stock
2 carrots, finely diced
3 sticks of celery, trimmed and
    finely chopped
6–8 nasturtium flowers

To serve
freshly grated Parmesan cheese
4–6 nasturtium flowers

Golden chicken cobbler

This recipe is another version of my favourite cobbler, a meat casserole topped with tender, scone-like dumplings. I like to make it in the summer when there are plenty of young vegetables about, not to mention marigolds and nasturtiums for the cobbler topping. You can use either boneless chicken breasts or thighs, or a mixture of the two, depending on whether you prefer white or darker meat. Cut into cubes of about 5 cm/2 inches. If using thighs, remove the meat from the bone and, before you start cooking the dish, make a little chicken stock with the thigh bones, any other trimmings, including the skin, a stick of sliced celery and a small piece of onion.

Fry the shallots and chicken to a golden brown in a lidded, oven-proof casserole. Sprinkle on the flour and stir it in to absorb any extra oil. Add a quarter of the wine and bring to the boil, stirring up any residues in the pan.

Pour in the rest of the wine and the stock, add the bay leaf and bring to the boil, cover and reduce the heat. Simmer gently for 20 minutes, then add the vegetables and cook for a further 20 to 30 minutes, until the vegetables are tender. Courgettes, corn kernels and mushrooms will, of course, take much less cooking and should be added towards the end.

To make the cobbler, crush the petals with the salt in a mortar and pestle. Sift the flour and baking powder, cut in the fat and then rub together. Add the crushed petals and stir in enough buttermilk or yoghurt to bind the mixture to a soft dough. Roll out to about 2.5 cm/1 inch thick and cut into rounds about 5-8 cm/2–3 inches in diameter.

Remove the lid from the casserole, arrange the scones round the top and bake for about 15 minutes in an oven pre-heated to 180°C/350° F/gas mark 4. Serve from the casserole, using marigold petals and whole nasturtiums as decoration.

serves 6 to 8

12 shallots
1–1.25 kg/2–2½ lb boneless chicken, prepared as described
2 tablespoons sunflower oil
1 tablespoon plain flour
½ bottle dry white wine
150 ml/5 fl oz chicken stock
1 bay leaf

Vegetables
Prepare a selection from amongst the following, about 1 kg/2 lb in all:
green beans
broad beans
small carrots
sweetcorn
courgettes
small potatoes
button mushrooms

Golden cobbler
2 tablespoons marigold and nasturtium petals
½ teaspoon coarse sea salt
280 g/10 oz self-raising flour
1 teaspoon baking powder
85 g/3 oz lard or butter, chilled and diced
150 ml/5 fl oz buttermilk or plain yoghurt thinned with water to the consistency of cream

Tomato, melon and mozzarella salad with lime and nasturtium dressing

This recipe is best made in late summer, when tomatoes and melons are at their ripest. Honeydew, galia and cantaloupe or charentais melons offer a pleasing colour contrast.

Put the tomatoes in a bowl. Remove the seeds from the melons and, using a melon baller to scoop out their flesh, add it to the tomatoes. Peel the cucumber, halve it, discard the seeds, dice the flesh and add it to the tomatoes and melon.

Put the zest from the lime in a jug and stir in the honey, lime juice, vinegar, oil, shredded nasturtium leaves and seasoning.

Spoon the salad onto plates, with or without salad leaves. Arrange the mozzarella on top and spoon over the well-mixed dressing. Garnish with nasturtium flowers.

serves 6 to 8

175 g/6 oz each of yellow and red cherry, or plum tomatoes
2 or 3 kinds of melon
juice and pared zest of 1 lime
1 teaspoon clear honey
1 tablespoon cider vinegar
2 tablespoons finely chopped chervil, basil or mint
3 tablespoons walnut or hazelnut oil
300 g/10 oz mozzarella, diced
1 cucumber
nasturtium leaves and flowers
salt
pepper

'Succotash' with marigolds and nasturtiums

Both flowers are in bloom at the same time as we begin to receive the new season's home-grown vegetables, and here I combine them in a stunningly pretty dish based on a Native American dish using fresh corn.

Boil the potatoes and carrots for 5 minutes in a large pan of lightly salted water, then add the corn, peas and beans and cook for another 2 minutes. Tip all the vegetables into a colander and dunk briefly in very cold water to prevent them cooking any further.

When well drained, put the cooked vegetables in a large bowl with the tomatoes. Carefully fold in the mayonnaise, together with the marigold petals and 6 chopped nasturtium flowers.

Arrange the salad leaves on a platter, spoon the vegetables on top and garnish with the petals of the remaining marigold and the whole nasturtium flowers.

serves 6

6 Charlotte or other potatoes, peeled and diced
4 carrots, diced
kernels of corn cut from 3 cobs
200 g/7 oz shelled peas
200 g/7 oz shelled broad beans
4 ripe but firm tomatoes, peeled, seeded and diced small
250 ml/8 fl oz home-made mayonnaise
petals of 3 marigolds
1 whole marigold
9 nasturtium flowers
salad leaves

Glamorgan sausages

This is another excellent recipe that combines the two flowers, both of which have an affinity with cheese. These sausages make a perfect starter that appeals to vegetarians and meat-eaters alike, and you can also make miniature versions to serve as cocktail snacks.

Leeks are a traditional ingredient, but if they are unavailable you can substitute spring onions with no loss of taste. The flowers are not a traditional ingredient, but nevertheless just right.

Mix together the crumbs, cheese, leek or spring onion, flowers and seasoning. Stir one whole egg and the yolk of a second egg into the mixture, with as much milk as is needed to bind it together. Whisk the left-over egg white together with the white only from an additional egg to a froth on a plate and put the flour or breadcrumbs in another. Divide the cheese mixture into twenty portions and roll each one into small sausage shapes. Coat each one in the egg white and then in flour or breadcrumbs. Heat the butter and oil in a frying pan and fry for about 10 minutes until golden brown.

Serve hot, warm or cold. They are good with home-made tomato sauce, chutney or pickles. Larger versions can be served as a first course. If you can deep-fry them, these 'sausages' are even better.

makes 20

250 g / 8 oz fresh breadcrumbs
250 g / 8 oz grated Caerphilly or other semi-hard cheese
1 leek or 4 spring onions, trimmed and finely chopped
1 tablespoon chopped marigold petals
1 tablespoon chopped nasturtium petals – you can also include a leaf or two if you wish
1 teaspoon mustard powder
salt
pepper
nutmeg
about 5 tablespoons milk, but see the recipe
2 eggs plus 1 egg white
flour or breadcrumbs for coating
25 g / 1 oz butter
1 tablespoon olive oil

Flower-strewn midsummer salmon

This is an adaptation of a favourite recipe in which salmon is covered with nasturtiums, marigolds and other summer flowers rather than herbs. Cornflower petals and a few leaves of flat parsley give a colourful contrast to the finished dish.

Spread the butter all over the salmon and season it lightly. Place the flower petals and herbs all over the fish – the butter will help to anchor them.

Put the cider in a roasting bag, and then the salmon. Secure the bag tightly, place it on a roasting tray and roast for about 20 minutes in an oven pre-heated to 180°C/350°F/gas mark 4.

Remove the fish from the oven and let it rest until it reaches room temperature. Serve with a salad of new potatoes and a green leaf salad. You can strain off the cooking juices, reduce them and then use them to flavour a mayonnaise or a sauce made with crème fraîche to serve with the fish.

serves 4 to 6

1 kg/generous 2 lb salmon fillet,
    with skin and bones removed
50 g/2 oz unsalted butter,
    softened
salt
pepper
petals of 2 marigolds
8–10 nasturtium flowers
petals of 6 cornflowers
a dozen leaves of flat-leaf parsley
2–3 tablespoons dry cider

Salmon souchy

This is another salmon recipe I often make with herbs, but which adapts beautifully to summer flowers, especially the bright colours and flavours of nasturtium and marigolds. Very easy and quick to cook, this is a very old method of cooking salmon and has the same origins as the Belgian waterzooi.

Slice the salmon very thinly, season and put it to one side. Make a broth with the remaining ingredients and simmer for about 30 minutes. Have the soup plates very hot and lay the salmon pieces in them with the herbs on top. Pour the boiling broth through a sieve over the salmon and serve immediately, garnished with the flowers.

serves 4

500 g / 1 lb salmon fillet
salt
pepper
salmon bones and head
1 celery stalk
a few parsley stalks
2 or 3 tablespoons chopped
    chives
2 or 3 tarragon stalks or lovage
6 nasturtium leaves
500 ml / 18 fl oz water
250 ml / 9 fl oz dry white wine

To serve
marigold petals, nasturtium
    flowers, others such as
    cornflower or daisy petals, and
    a few tarragon leaves

Orange flowers, jasmine and linden blossom

All these blossoms bring with them hints of the warm south – a shaded patio in Andalusia, a scented Provençal garden, a village square in Sicily – and such is the depth of perfume that in each case you can transform it into creams, sorbets, jellies and numerous other dishes.

'The magical dishes she prepared filled the atmosphere around her with tantalising aromas: fragrant gum Arabic in rice pudding … custards scented with orange blossom water.'

Lian Badr, *Stars of Jericho*

Orange flowers

The blossoms used for orange flower water and other preparations are those of the bitter or Seville orange, best known to cooks in the British Isles for making marmalade. Neroli, the fragrant oil of the bitter orange, is used in perfumery and orange flower water is the scented by-product of the distilling process used to obtain the more costly oil.

During the eighteenth century Malta was the main supplier of oranges and orange flower water to France, and the crowned heads of Europe were accustomed to receiving both as gifts from the Knights of St John. Neroli was also produced, as well as jasmine *pommade* and a *pommade à la gazia*, an acacia flower, or mimosa, oil. A fascinating correspondence of the period between a Parisian grocer and his son, a young cleric attached to the Knights, shows an impatient father urging that the orange trees be watered just once a fortnight, that his son select only the very best oranges and that he pack them carefully in wood chips or wrapped in cotton. He even gives detailed instructions for making the crates in which the oranges were to be shipped. Sometimes he wants the neroli decanted from the orange flower water and sent separately, sometimes he says he will do this job himself. Very rarely is he satisfied with what his son sends. Orange flower water is still used today in traditional Maltese desserts, such as *mqaret*, *kwarezimal* and *figolli*, date-filled pastries, Lenten almond cakes and special biscuits eaten at Easter.

Although southern Spain is now Europe's main orange grove, orange flower water is surprisingly little used in Iberian cuisine, while in Sicily and southern Italy, where traces of Arabic irrigation systems can still be seen, this fragrant water is found only rarely in the kitchen. Instead, one has to look south to Morocco, or further east.

There are, however, many old English recipes using orange flower water, a number of which deserve to be revived, especially as good quality orange flower water is increasingly available in food halls, some supermarket specialty sections and, of course, in Middle Eastern shops.

Fairy butter

I suggest this traditional eighteenth-century recipe as an alternative to clotted cream when you are serving warm scones for tea. It is also good with griddle cakes, crumpets and other similarly nostalgic tea breads.

Pound the egg yolks with the liquid and the icing sugar, then mix them thoroughly with the butter. When well mixed, let the butter firm up slightly in the refrigerator and then push it through a sieve onto a small plate, letting it fall loosely in a heap.

makes about 100 g/4 oz

yolks of 2 large hard-boiled eggs
1 tablespoon orange flower water
1 tablespoon icing sugar
50 g/2 oz unsalted butter,
    at room temperature

Orange flower liqueur

I make this in the same way that I make *limoncello*, but can only make it where I am able to gather fresh orange blossoms, which, sadly, is very rarely. Instead of thinly pared lemon zest, I fill a wide-mouthed, flask-shaped decanter with fresh orange blossoms, about 250 g/8 or 9 oz, together with a crushed cardamom pod and 5 cumin seeds. I then pour on as much vodka or plain *eau de vie* as the decanter will hold, seal the top with cling film and leave it on a sunny windowsill or another warm spot for at least three weeks.

Just before I am ready to bottle it, I make a simple syrup, boiling an equal volume of sugar and water, say 500 g to ½ litre, and then let it cool. I strain the flavoured syrup into a large jug, mix it thoroughly with the syrup and pour it into sterilised bottles, which I then seal and label. Like all these fragrant preparations, this is best stored either in a cool dark place or in the freezer. It makes a stunning *digestif*, and I also use it to flavour orange sorbets, mandarin ice-cream, soufflés and fillings for crepes or sponge cakes.

Orange flower macaroons

Inspired by the eighteenth-century cooks and their flower water recipes, this is nevertheless a modern recipe for the classic French *macaron*, which I was taught to make by a French *pâtissier* some years ago.

Sift the ground almonds and measured sugar together: they must be absolutely smooth and fine. Whisk the egg whites and, as they firm up, sprinkle in the powdered egg white and the tablespoon of sugar, whisking until the mixture is very firm, smooth and glossy. Add some of the almond and sugar mixture to the egg white and fold in gently, and then the remaining dry ingredients and the orange zest. The mixture should have the consistency of soft paste and remain glossy and smooth.

Pipe into small mounds, about 2–3 cm / 1 inch apart, on non-stick baking sheets. Let the macaroons dry for 20 to 30 minutes before baking for 4 minutes at 150°C/300°F/gas mark 3. Turn the tray around and cook for another 4 minutes.

Allow to cool, then sandwich with the following mixture.

makes about 40

125 g / generous 4 oz ground almonds
225 g / 8 oz icing sugar, plus an additional tablespoon
100 ml / 4 fl oz egg white (4 or 5)
1 teaspoon dried egg white powder (optional)
2 teaspoons very finely pared orange zest

Orange flower cream

As well as providing the perfect complement to orange flower macaroons, this also makes an excellent filling for sponge cakes.

Whisk all the ingredients together until just firm enough to use as a filling.

200 ml / 7 fl oz double cream
1 tablespoon finely pared orange zest
2 tablespoons icing sugar
2 tablespoons orange flower water

Orange flower roulade with dates, pistachios and ricotta

I developed this recipe after a visit to Marrakech, where the scent of orange blossom in the gardens was so strong that it woke me up in the morning.

Whisk half the sugar and the egg yolks in a bowl set in a pan over – but not touching – simmering water until they are pale and foamy and the mixture leaves a ribbon when trailed on the surface.

Use a clean whisk to beat the egg whites with the remaining sugar until firm and glossy. Fold together the yolk mixture, flour and egg whites, adding the orange zest and orange flower water.

Line a Swiss roll tin with buttered greaseproof paper and pour in the mixture. Smooth the surface and bake in an oven pre-heated to 180°C/350°F/gas mark 4 for 12 minutes, or until the sponge begins to shrink away from the side of the tin.

Remove from the oven, turn the sponge out flat onto a damp clean tea-towel and carefully peel off the paper. Trim off the crusty edges and roll up the cake with the damp tea-towel. Leave it to one side while you prepare the filling.

Blend the ricotta, honey and orange flower water, and stir in the dates and pistachios. Unroll the sponge, spread with the filling and re-roll it. Serve the same day, dusted with icing sugar.

serves 6

Sponge
100 g/4 oz unrefined caster sugar
3 eggs, separated
100 g/4 oz plain flour, sifted
pared zest of 1 orange
2 tablespoons orange flower water

Filling
200 g/7 oz fresh ricotta
2 tablespoons date syrup or honey
a few drops of orange flower water
12 dates, stoned and chopped
2–3 tablespoons pistachios,
    shelled and unsalted

Winter jam

Instead of the traditional mincemeat for Christmas, I sometimes use some of the same ingredients to make a Christmas jam. Rather than being bound with suet, the dried fruit is suspended in apple, or – if you can get it – quince jelly. The jam is even more versatile than mincemeat, in that it is delicious on toast, muffins or scones, and you can also use it in tarts and pies. It is especially good when combined with almond paste. Quinces are imported from Turkey in the early autumn and are available in Middle Eastern and Turkish shops, and occasionally in supermarkets and food halls.

Cut the Bramleys or quinces into wedges and simmer in the water in a large saucepan until soft. Press with a potato masher and then drip the pulp through a jelly bag, preferably overnight, into a bowl containing the dried pears, which should be cut into very thin slivers. There will be about 1.3 litres / 2 pints of liquid.

Stone the rest of the dried fruit as necessary and cut it all into small dice or thin slivers. Put everything except for the nuts into the apple extract with the soaked pears. Stir well and simmer gently until the sugar has dissolved. Bring to a full boil and cook for 5 minutes. Skim the surface and add the nuts. Boil for a further 5 minutes until the mixture jells and then pot in clean, hot jars. Seal, label and date.

makes about six 400 g / 1/2 lb jars

1.5 kg / 3 lb Bramleys or quinces
1.5 litres / 2 1/2 pints water
200 g / 7 oz dried pears

200 g / 7 oz dried figs
200 g / 7 oz dried apricots
100 g / 3 1/2 oz dates
100 g / 3 1/2 oz dried mango
50 g / 2 oz candied lemon peel
50 g / 2 oz candied orange peel
50 g / 2 oz angelica
juice and finely pared zest of
    1 orange
juice and finely pared zest of
    1 lemon
4–6 tablespoons orange flower
    water
1/2 teaspoon ground cardamom
1/2 teaspoon ground cinnamon
1/2 teaspoon ground anis
1 kg / 2 lb preserving sugar
150 g / 5 oz walnut pieces
150 g / 5 oz flaked almonds

Orange salad

This is a lovely dessert to serve in winter when citrus fruit is plentiful. It is a particularly good dish for the holiday season, when not everyone wants rich Christmas pudding and mince pies.

Peel the fruit and slice or divide into segments as appropriate – it is better to have a mixture of shapes. Try to remove as much pith and skin as possible. Put the fruit in a glass bowl, together with any juice squeezed from the end slices. Sift the icing sugar over the fruit to bring out more juice, then add the flower waters. Chill until required and scatter on the almonds just before serving. You might want to add a dash of lime juice if the oranges are very sweet.

serves 6

1.5 kg / 3 lb of mandarins, clementines, navel oranges, ortaniques and any other sweet citrus fruit you can find
1 tablespoon icing sugar
1 tablespoon rosewater
2–3 tablespoons orange flower water
3 tablespoons toasted flaked almonds

Pomegranate and orange flower water salad

If you come across really beautiful pomegranates, large, heavy and with ruby red interiors, prepare them this way for a simple, exquisite and refreshing dessert. Carefully pull the fruit away from the leathery pith and pile it in a shallow glass dish. Sprinkle with orange flower water and sift a light snow of icing sugar on top. Chill before serving.

Cook's tip

Pomegranates flavoured with rosewater are also delicious, and I have served a very similar salad as a savoury, adding sliced or diced cucumber, some herbs, a vinaigrette and no sugar.

Orange-scented salmon with couscous

This is inspired by a famous Fassi recipe collected by Madame Guinaudeau, who described the cooking of Fez in her stylish *Traditional Moroccan Cooking*. Her recipe is for a whole stuffed shad, which is cooked for several hours, and I have adapted the method to use salmon fillets. Anyone who has ever wrestled with bony shad fillets will appreciate the wisdom of lengthy cooking, which helps to 'dissolve' the bones. This recipe, on the other hand, is quickly cooked, and is best made with rectangular pieces of salmon fillet. If you can't find *ras el hanout*, a teaspoon each of crushed cardamom, cumin and coriander seeds will serve as a substitute.

Using a sharp knife, make a pocket in each salmon piece to hold the stuffing. Season the fish all over lightly with *ras el hanout*, salt and pepper.

Gently fry the shallots in oil until soft and then stir in the remaining spice mixture. Cook for 3 or 4 minutes, remove from the heat and add the rest of the ingredients. When cool, spoon the mixture into the salmon pockets.

Moisten the couscous with a few tablespoons of water and, when it has been absorbed, break up the couscous with your fingers and put it in a sieve to steam over hot water. If you are using instant couscous, simply follow the instructions on the packet.

When the couscous is just tender, stir in the rest of the ingredients. Prepare the leaves by rolling them and cutting into shreds with a sharp knife.

To finish the salmon, heat the butter in a large frying pan and place the fish in it, top side down. Turn the pieces over after 1 minute and continue cooking for 5 to 8 minutes, depending on thickness. You can cover the pan so that the fish steams a little. Remove the fish and keep it warm, then raise the heat under the frying pan and reduce the fish stock by between a third and a half.

serves 6

6 x 175 g/6 oz pieces of salmon fillet, skinned
1 tablespoon *ras el hanout*
salt
pepper
2–3 shallots, finely chopped
1 tablespoon sunflower or groundnut oil
12 dates, stoned and chopped
2 tablespoons orange flower water
2 tablespoons fresh mint, finely chopped
pared zest of 1 lemon
2–3 teaspoons lemon juice

Couscous
250 g/8 oz couscous
3 tomatoes, seeded and chopped
50 g/2 oz spinach, rocket or watercress
1 tablespoon mint leaves, finely chopped
2–3 tablespoons lightly toasted pine kernels, unsalted pistachios or flaked almonds
salt
pepper

To finish
25 g/1 oz unsalted butter
450 ml/16 fl oz fish stock, made from the salmon bones
a small bunch of fresh coriander

Orange-scented salmon with couscous /continued

Spoon a base of couscous into large soup plates and place the fish fillets on top. Arrange several sprigs of coriander around the bowl and pour a little boiling stock over it. The salmon can be garnished with more coriander or finely chopped unsalted pistachios.

Grilled fruit skewers

This is a dessert for winter, when we have to rely on imported fruit. You can also make this with mango, pineapple and guava.

This recipe needs to be started the day before you plan to serve it, as the dried apricots have to be soaked overnight in the orange juice and orange flower water.

Cut the sharon fruit into 8 wedges and then thread with the rest of the fruit onto two wooden skewers, first soaked in orange flower water. If there is any soaking liquid left from the apricots, brush it all over the fruit. Spread a thin layer of icing sugar on a piece of wax paper or a plate and roll the fruit skewers in it until well-coated. Ensure that the grill is very hot and put the skewers under it for a few minutes, turning them once or twice, just until the edges of the fruit begin to caramelise.

Serve alone, or as an accompaniment to dark or white chocolate mousse, or alongside a wedge of ricotta, a dollop of mascarpone or a scoop of ice-cream or sorbet. A syrup flavoured with orange flower water and Curaçao also goes well.

serves 2

6 dried apricots
75 ml / 3 fl oz fresh orange juice
2 tablespoons orange flower water
1 sharon fruit
8 kumquats
10 physallis, husked
icing sugar

Orange and almond tart

The combination of oranges, orange flower water and almonds always reminds me of Andalusia.

Mix the butter, sugar, almonds and seasoning until you have a soft mass. Work in the flour and egg, gather the pastry into a ball, cover it with cling film and let it rest in the refrigerator for about 30 minutes.

Lightly beat the egg yolks with the mandarin or orange juice and zest and the orange flower water. Cream the butter and sugar, then mix in with the egg yolks, flour and almonds. Whisk the egg whites and gently fold them in with the rest of the ingredients.

Roll out the pastry and use it to line a 23–25 cm / 9–10 inch quiche dish or tart ring. Prick the base all over, cover with foil or greaseproof paper, weigh down with baking beans and bake for 15 minutes in an oven pre-heated to 180°C/350°F/gas mark 4.

Remove from the oven and allow to cool slightly before spooning in the filling. If you wish, the tart can be baked blind the day before required. Smooth the surface of the filling and bake at 180°C/350°F/gas mark 4 for 35 to 40 minutes until the filling is just set and golden. About 10 minutes before the end of baking, scatter flaked almonds or pieces of crystallised orange peel over the filling.

serves 6 to 8

Orange and almond pastry
100 g / 4 oz unsalted butter, softened
50 g / 2 oz icing sugar
25 g / 1 oz ground almonds
a pinch of salt
1 tablespoon orange flower water
1 tablespoon grated orange zest
250 g / 8 oz plain flour
1 egg, lightly beaten

Filling
4 egg yolks
juice and pared zest of
    2 mandarins or oranges
3 tablespoons orange flower water
100 g / 4 oz unsalted butter, at
    room temperature
100 g / 4 oz caster sugar
25 g / 1 oz plain flour, sifted
75 g / 3 oz ground almonds
2 egg whites, whisked

Garnish
flaked almonds or crystallised orange peel

Orange, onion and olive salad

In Morocco this is usually served as part of an array of fragrant and piquant salads served at the beginning of a meal. Orange flower water is used to flavour many of them, including one of small lettuces, simply quartered, sprinkled with the fragrant water and a little olive oil. Carrot, cucumber and even tomato salads are flavoured with orange flower water. I strongly recommend you try incorporating it into a vinaigrette.

Peel and slice the oranges into a bowl, squeezing in the juices from the end slices. Peel and thinly slice the onion and add it to the oranges, together with the remaining ingredients. Mix gently and then season lightly.

serves 4

3 navel oranges
1 mild (preferably white) onion
3 tablespoons pitted olives, black, green or mixed
1 tablespoon orange flower water
2 tablespoons extra virgin olive oil
salt
pepper
fresh coriander or mint leaves to garnish

'White coffee'

This could not be simpler to make, and I recommend it highly, although it is not coffee at all, but a perfect *digestif* after a meal: just hot water, slightly sweetened and flavoured with orange flower water. I first tasted 'white coffee' with a Kuwaiti family at their beach house. We had driven down the coast road from Kuwait City, a modern beach development on one side, a camel train stepping through the desert sand on the other. The lunch was magical, olives and dates from the family's own groves, exquisite dishes of chicken and fish, duck and quail, each served with rice, flavoured and garnished in the appropriate way for the main ingredient. Sweet, sticky pastries and black coffee were taken at small tables, men separate from women, and when we finally left the dining room, small cups of 'white coffee' were brought to us on the terrace by the beach.

Warm small coffee cups and put a spoonful of orange flower water and a sugar lump in each. Fill the cups with water that has just come off the boil. If the orange flower water is strong and fragrant, a teaspoonful will do, otherwise you may need to add more.

Jasmine

There is a certain amount of confusion surrounding jasmine. The flower I refer to is the white, star-like, highly scented *Jasminum officinale*. The larger flower, normally found in southern regions like Andalusia, is the *Jasminum grandiflora*. Both belong to the Oleaceae family and both are edible. Jasmine has been used in the traditional medicine of many cultures as a calmative and an aphrodisiac, and also as a cure for coughs.

'Jasmine is sweet and has many loves.'

Thomas Hood, *Flowers*

Two other flowers with similar names have no place in the kitchen. Cape Jasmine or *Gardenia hasminoidis*, a member of the Gardenia family, **is not edible**. Yellow or Carolina Jasmine, *Gelsemium sempervirens*, is a **poisonous** member of the Loganaceae family.

An important part of the parfumier's canon, jasmine should be treated by the cook in the same way. It is a rewarding flower to work with as it is so highly scented, but it is also delicate and must be picked early in the morning before the essential oils evaporate.

It is well worth gathering jasmine flowers to dry for future use in teas and tisanes, and for steeping in cream or syrup.

Jasmine-flavoured lobster stew

Shellfish has an affinity with 'sweet' flavours such as vanilla and jasmine, and I like to combine it with both lobster and crab.

The secret to a lobster stew is the maturing process. Unlike most shellfish dishes, this is best made well in advance, as I learned from cooks in Maine, who know everything there is to know about lobsters. While two days is said to improve it hugely, you can eat this stew within 6 or 7 hours. It must, of course, be cooled quickly, refrigerated and thoroughly reheated before serving.

Take the coral and tomally, the soft, pale-green creamy flesh, and gently cook this in the butter in a heavy saucepan for 5 to 10 minutes, breaking up the coral with the back of a spoon. Cut the lobster tail meat into large chunks and add them to the pan to cook for a further 10 minutes. Remove from the heat and allow to cool for 15 to 20 minutes. Scald the milk with the jasmine and then add gradually to the lobster, stirring continuously and no more than a trickle at a time. During the stirring, the stew should turn a delicate, pale salmon colour. When all the milk has been added, cool the stew quickly, setting the saucepan in a bowl of ice if possible. Cover, and then refrigerate until required.

(serves 1-2)

1 small lobster, lightly and freshly cooked and still warm, weighing about 750g–1 kg/ 1½–2 lb
50 g/2 oz butter
300 ml/½ pint full-cream milk
15 g/½ oz jasmine flowers
salt
pepper

Lychees in jasmine syrup

We can now buy lychees throughout the year, so it is possible to use fresh jasmine to make this simple yet exquisite fruit salad. I used to make it only during the winter, with jasmine tea. This meant I would plunder most of the dried flowers from the tea, which of course ceased to be jasmine tea.

Put the flowers and thinly pared lemon zest into a bowl. Boil the water, pour it over the flowers and

serves 4

40 g/1½ oz fresh jasmine flowers
zest and juice of half a lemon
250 ml/8 fl oz boiling water
200 g/7 oz granulated sugar
750 g/½ lb lychees

leave to infuse until cold. Stir in the sugar, bring to the boil gently until the sugar has dissolved and then cook for 5 minutes, adding as much lemon juice as you like to sharpen the syrup, taking care not to mask the fragrance and flavour of the jasmine. Remove from the heat and allow to cool.

Peel and stone the fruit carefully and place in a glass bowl. Pour some of the syrup over the fruit and serve at once or keep it cool until required. Save the rest of the syrup for another bowl of lychees, as you will want to make it again. This is the perfect dessert to serve at the end of an oriental meal.

Fresh jasmine, green tea and almond jelly

This is an easy and inexpensive jelly to make in the summer when the jasmine is in full bloom.

Put the tea and flowers in separate tea bags in a large jug and pour on 1 litre/36 fl oz boiling water. Remove the tea after 30 minutes, but leave the flowers to steep for an hour.

Strain the liquid into a saucepan. Stir in the sugar and cook gently until the sugar has dissolved. Then bring to a rapid boil until setting point is reached – this only takes about 4 minutes. Skim the surface and allow to stand for a few minutes before stirring in the almonds and almond essence.

Pour into the prepared jars, cover with wax discs and cellophane covers and label.

makes about 2.5 kg/5 lb

1 oz/25 g green tea
75 g/3 oz fresh jasmine flowers
1 kg/36 oz preserving sugar
75 g/3 oz blanched flaked
   almonds
1/2 teaspoon pure almond essence

Mango, almond and jasmine crumble

The heady scent of jasmine marries far better with lush, tropical fruits than with berry fruits. Here, not too ripe mangoes are diced and baked in individual pots with a crunchy topping of almond, jasmine flowers and sugar, which also flavours the jasmine custard served with the pudding. I suggest you make the custard in advance.

Use a little of the butter to grease a flan or soufflé dish. Peel and dice the mangoes, discarding the stones, then toss the fruit in lemon juice and sprinkle it with 2–3 tablespoons of sugar so that a good syrup is produced.

Put the fruit in the dish and dot it with another 25 g / 1 oz of the butter. Rub the remaining butter into the flour until it resembles fine breadcrumbs. Grind the remaining sugar with the jasmine flowers and stir lightly into the flour and butter mixture, together with half the almonds. Spoon the crumble mixture on top of the fruit, pressing it down a little.

Bake in an oven pre-heated to 180°C/350°F/gas mark 4 for about 30 minutes, until the crumble topping is golden, scattering the rest of the flaked almonds on the surface for the last 10 minutes.

serves 6

175 g / 6 oz unsalted butter
2 large mangoes
juice of 1 lemon
175 g / 6 oz golden granulated sugar
175 g / 6 oz plain flour
1½ tablespoons fresh or 2 teaspoons dried jasmine flowers
75 g / 3 oz flaked almonds

Jasmine custard

Scald the cream, pour it over the jasmine flowers and leave until cold. Beat the egg yolks in another bowl set over a pan of simmering water or the top part of a bain-marie and strain the cream over them. Cook gently until the mixture coats the back of a spoon, but without letting it curdle. Sweeten to taste and put to one side until required. Keep the custard closely covered with cling film to stop a skin forming.

300 ml / ½ pint single cream
40 g / 1½ oz fresh jasmine flowers
4 egg yolks
sugar to taste

Cook's tip

This crumble is also delicious made with guavas.

Linden blossom

Scents often help me to recall
a place far more vividly than a photograph –
for example when I smell linden flowers on a hot
summer day, I invariably remember standing under a
linden tree in Piana degli Albanesi, a hill town about
an hour's drive from Palermo. I have never before or
since come across such large and fragrant blossoms,
yet I was not in this strange town long enough to find
out whether any local use was made of the blossom. I
certainly came across no intriguing bottles of liqueur
nor unusual ice-cream flavours, in either of which the
blossom might have been expected to make an
appearance. The *cannoli*, on the other hand, were
clearly a speciality – I have never seen so many being
consumed on a Sunday morning. Visiting friends
elsewhere in Italy, they were surprised when they saw
me gathering linden flowers, which they did not even
use for infusions, although they rather liked those I
made for them.

Linden flower, or *tilleul*, is much used in France for
tisanes and infusions, as well as stronger drinks. *Ratafia
de tilleul* used to be made in the Drôme, where the
most fragrant French blossoms come from. When I
was a teacher at the Ecole Normale in Albi, the
surveillantes, assistant housekeeper and I would often
brew up a large pot of *tilleul* and sit around in the
infirmerie for an hour's gossip before bed – and yes,
occasionally, one of us would buy a bag of *madeleines*…

Do try these fragrant flowers in the kitchen – they are
easy and rewarding to use, coming into bloom in
June, just after elderflowers, and are available dried at

*'If thou lookest on the
lime leaf
Thou a heart's form will
discover
Therefore are the lindens ever
Chosen seats for each fond
lover.'*

Heinrich Heine, *Book of Songs*

other times of the year. If you know of a linden tree, it is well worth harvesting the blossom and drying it for use throughout the year.

Tilia cordata and *T.platyphyllos* produce the most fragrant flowers, ideal for tisanes, but also for flavouring delicate creams, syrups and sorbets. It makes a delicious addition to summer food, and I also like it with fish dishes, especially salmon trout. Lime blossom is also an interesting flavouring for white meats, stocks and cream sauces, using white wine or cider as the base. So whilst infusions, creams and ices are its most common uses, there are many other dishes to be enhanced with this delicate scent.

Linden flower ice-cream

This is a most subtly flavoured ice-cream. I sometimes use honey rather than sugar as a sweetener, which can work well, but not here, as it will overpower the delicate flavour of the linden blossoms.

Simmer the flowers in the syrup for 5 minutes and, removing the pan from the heat, leave to infuse until cool. You can happily leave this overnight.

Scald the milk in a separate saucepan, remove from the heat and stir in the scented syrup. Again, leave to infuse until cool and only then strain. Scald the cream and pour on the egg yolks, whisking all the time. Return the saucepan to a very gentle heat and stir the custard continuously until it thickens slightly. Combine the custard with the flavoured mixture and, when cool, freeze in the usual way.

makes 1 litre

a good handful of linden flowers, about 40 g / 1½ oz
250 ml / 8 fl oz sugar syrup
375 ml / 13 fl oz full-cream milk
250 ml / 8 fl oz whipping cream
4 egg yolks, lightly beaten

Almond *panna cotta* with apricots and linden flower syrup

Essentially a cream jelly rather than cooked cream, this is an exquisitely rich, silky pudding, perfect for a festive summer occasion.

Heat the milk to boiling point. Put the almonds in the bowl of a food-processor, briefly process until they are just broken and then pour on the milk. Allow to cool to room temperature and then process until the almonds and milk are completely blended. Strain the mixture through a fine cloth, then twist it until all the liquid is extracted: this is your almond milk. Do not discard the ground almonds – you can use them in a cake or tart.

Soften the gelatine in a little water and then drain it. Heat the cream to blood temperature, then add the sugar, almond essence (if you are using it) and drained gelatine. Stir until dissolved and then allow the cream to cool. Pour it into a wet pudding basin or jelly mould before the mixture begins to set and then refrigerate overnight.

Halve the apricots and poach them in a little water with the linden flowers secured in a filter bag or piece of muslin. Transfer the fruit to a large, shallow serving dish. Add sugar in the proportion of half the volume of liquid, stir until dissolved, then simmer for 2 to 3 minutes. Remove from the heat and allow to cool.

To serve, loosen the *panna cotta* by holding a hot cloth to the mould or dipping it briefly in hot water, and carefully turn out onto the serving dish, surrounded by apricot halves. Pour the linden syrup over the cream and fruit. If you have fresh linden flowers, they will look very pretty around the dish.

serves 8

200 g / 7 oz almonds, blanched
    and skinned
300 ml / 1/2 pint full-cream milk
4 sheets gelatine or 4 teaspoons
    powdered gelatine
600 ml / 20 fl oz double cream
caster sugar to taste
a dash of pure almond essence
    to taste
1 kg / 2 lb apricots
40 g / 1 1/2 oz fresh or 20 g / 3/4 oz
    dried linden flowers
water
sugar (see recipe)

Linden flower and lime sorbet with white chocolate galettes

Although linden flowers make a heavenly tisane, on their own they are too delicately flavoured to form the basis for a sorbet. Anything frozen needs heightened flavour, which here is provided by the lime.

Thinly peel the zest off the lime and put it in a jug with the linden flowers. Pour on the boiling water and leave to infuse for 10 minutes. Stir in the lime juice and sugar and, when this has dissolved, strain the infusion, cool and freeze in an ice-cream maker or freezer container.

Break up the chocolate, put it in a small heatproof glass jug and stand it in very hot water until the chocolate has melted, or melt it in a microwave. Pour the chocolate onto a sheet of greaseproof paper or lightly oiled marble slab, a drop at a time, and allow it to spread to thin discs. When set, peel off the paper, or carefully remove from the slab, and serve with the sorbet.

serves 2

1 lime
2 tablespoons linden flowers
200 ml / 7 fl oz water
100 g / 4 oz granulated sugar, or more to taste
75 g / 3 oz white chocolate

Poached salmon in linden flower jelly

This is a very adaptable recipe, for salmon steaks for two, a whole fish or a fillet. As it is a cold dish, it is perfect for entertaining. The recipe below is based on a small whole salmon or grilse weighing about 1.5 kg / 3 lb. Alternatively, you can use a sea trout. If you cook two salmon steaks, reduce the liquids by about two-thirds, adapting the rest of the ingredients accordingly.

Simmer all the ingredients in a saucepan for 45 minutes and then strain them into a wide, shallow pan or frying pan.

Put a second handful of linden flowers into a jug, pour on 200 ml / 7 fl oz court bouillon and leave to

serves 6 to 8

Court bouillon
600 ml / 20 fl oz dry white wine
600 ml / 20 fl oz water
40 g / 1½ oz linden flowers
1 celery stalk, chopped
thinly pared zest of 1 lemon
2 bay leaves
1 sprig of tarragon
1 sprig of thyme
a handful of parsley stalks
1 teaspoon peppercorns
2 teaspoons salt

steep. The court bouillon should be boiling and the mixture left to steep while the fish is cooking.

To poach the salmon, carefully lower the fish into the boiling court bouillon, which will immediately go off the boil. Lower the heat and bring the liquid gently back to just under simmering point, the water should tremble but bubbles not break the surface. Thick fish steaks should be poached for about 10 minutes, fillets for about 5 to 8 minutes and whole fish for 10 minutes for each 2.5 cm/1 inch of thickness at the deepest part. Remove the fish carefully, drain it on a clean tea-towel or kitchen paper and then transfer to a rack to cool. If poaching a very large fish, you will need to make double or triple the quantity of court bouillon.

To make 600 ml/20 fl oz jelly, strain the liquid in which you have cooked the fish through a sieve lined with wet muslin into a saucepan or large jug. Measure out just over 450 ml/16 fl oz and put in a jug. Stir in the softened gelatine until it has dissolved and add the linden infusion. Season the liquid to taste, bearing in mind that as it cools the flavour will weaken. Lay the fish in a terrine, ring mould, jelly mould or soup plates. Add any herbs, spices or other garnish and spoon on the cold liquid. Cover carefully and refrigerate until set.

Flavouring
a handful of linden flowers

Gelatine
Allow 4 sheets or 4 teaspoons powdered gelatine for each 600 ml/20 fl oz of liquid. Before adding it to the hot liquid, soften the gelatine first in a little cold water in a bowl, deducting it from the total amount of liquid required.

Cook's tip

You can adapt this recipe to use skate, sole fillets, scallops or a mixture of white fish and shellfish.

Summer vegetable risotto

An infusion of flowers provides some of the cooking liquid for the rice, which enhances the flavour of the vegetables in a most subtle manner. I find a deep, heavy frying pan is best for cooking risotto.

Put the flowers and wine in a saucepan, bring to the boil, remove from the heat and leave to infuse for 5 minutes or so.

Fry the shallots for 4 to 5 minutes in the olive oil, without letting them brown, and then stir in the rice until it is well coated in oil. Boil the stock separately in another saucepan. Pour a ladle of wine through a strainer over the rice, stir well and, when the wine has been absorbed by the rice, add the rest of it, also strained. When this, too, has been absorbed, add the stock, a little at a time, allowing the rice to absorb it before adding more. With the first batch of stock, add the chopped asparagus, except for the tips, and then after 5 minutes or so, half the grated courgettes, then the remaining courgettes and the asparagus tips about 10 minutes later, and finally the peas just before the rice is ready. Stir the risotto from time to time.

The rice may be cooked to your liking before you have used up all the stock. I like my risotto quite soft, moist and creamy, rather than dry. Just before serving, stir in the oil and the Parmesan cheese.

serves 4 to 6

250 ml/8 fl oz dry white wine
30 g/1 oz linden flowers
2 shallots, chopped
2 tablespoons extra virgin olive oil
350 g/12 oz arborio, carnaroli or vialone rice
up to 1 litre/2 pints vegetable stock
8 asparagus spears, trimmed and chopped
2 courgettes, topped, tailed and grated
a handful of frozen peas
salt
pepper

To serve
extra virgin olive oil
freshly grated Parmesan cheese

Roses

Roses have been used in the kitchen at least since
Roman times, when their petals were used to flavour
wine. Later, Arab pharmacists used roses to make syrups,
cordials and tonics, while the great Persian physician
Avicenna is said to have made the first rosewater in
the tenth century, and the use of flower waters spread
throughout those parts of southern Europe conquered
by the Arabs, particularly the Iberian peninsula.

The Catalan work, *El Libre del Coch* by Mestre Robert
(or Ruperto) de Nola, cook to King Ferdinand I of
Naples, published in Barcelona in 1520, has a recipe
for figs with rose petals included by Barbara Santich in
The Original Mediterranean Cuisine. Dried figs are
layered with rose petals and sugar and kept sealed in a
jar for between 15 and 20 days, until ready to eat.
This practice is not dissimilar to one still followed in
various Mediterranean countries, where figs are
packed with fragrant leaves such as bay or myrtle.

At about the same time that *El Libre de Coch* first
appeared, dried rose petals pounded to a powder were
included in the elaborate melange of spices used in
the preparation of drinking chocolate in Spain. Dried
rose petals are still used in China to flavour tea,
notably the delicate rose congou, a black oolong best
taken without milk or lemon.

By the late sixteenth century, English recipe
collections included the use of roses for medicinal,

*'The rose looks fair, but fairer
we it deem,
For that sweet odour which
doth in it live.'*
William Shakespeare,
Sonnet LIV

household and culinary usage, particularly rose-
infused oil, syrup of damask roses and rose conserve.

Persian cooking made considerable use of roses and
rosewater, and the Moghuls brought this tradition
with them to India, where it became part of the
country's courtly cooking. Joyce Westrip's *Moghul
Cooking* includes a recipe for rose-scented raisin
chutney, a delightfully fresh and piquant condiment
combining raisins, chilli, fresh ginger, cumin, lime
juice and rose essence. This *chatni* reminds me of the
lively sambals I enjoyed in Sri Lanka, where fresh
herbs, vegetables, fruit and chillies are chopped, mixed
and served raw, rather than those chutneys that are
cooked to a spicy jamminess. Rose petals are also used
in a rich Kashmiri pilau, in which the rice is cooked
in cream flavoured with the 'sweet' spices of cloves,
cinnamon and cardamom as well as cumin and bay
leaves. Rosewater perfumes a Hyderabadi biryani that
combines nuts, dried fruit, mint, coriander, potatoes
and carrots in a soothing vegetarian rice dish, and it is
also used to flavour desserts such as faluda and halva.

The most modern, not to say futuristic, use of roses in
the kitchen I have experienced is a dish developed by
Ferran Adrià, of El Bulli in Catalonia, who is regarded
by his peers as one of the world's most creative chefs.
I was privileged to watch him make the rosewater
bubbles that he serves floating in a lychee soup on
which fresh rose petals are scattered. It is far beyond
the scope of this book to go into the details of Adrià's
method, which involves mixing rosewater with sugar
and lecithin for stability, putting it in a soda siphon
and squirting out streams of foam into a bowl of
water. These are then separated into smaller sections
with the fingers. Gradually the foam clears and all that
is left is a bubble. These are carefully lifted out of the
water and transferred to the lychee soup. When you
bite into it, you experience the merest breath of roses.

One line of instruction in rose petal recipes has always
puzzled me, and I thought I had found the answer in
Constance Spry, who wrote that scented, modern
roses were suitable for use in the kitchen, but need to

be shredded and 'the hard base of the petal is cut away', while the texture of old-fashioned roses was thin enough that they could be used whole. Yet every rose recipe in the seventeenth-century *Book of Fruit and Flowers* also instructs the reader to 'clip off all the white'. On the other hand, neither John Nott in his 1723 *Cooks and Confectioners' Dictionary* nor Sir Hugh Platt in *Delights for Ladies,* published in 1594, gives this instruction. I have made all the recipes that follow without clipping the rose petals and I find that neither colour nor flavour is impaired.

However, rose petals will not soften if you cook them in syrup. The best way to deal with them in jelly making is to let the hot liquid drip through the muslin onto the rose petals, which will cause them to wilt, if not cook, and then bring the liquid and petals to the boil before adding the sugar.

The best roses to use are those at the deep pink to dark red end of the spectrum, and should come from one of the old-fashioned scented varieties, such as *Rosa officinalis*, the apothecary's rose, *R. gallica*, *R. damascena* and *R. centifolia*.

Taffety tart

This recipe, with its exquisite combination of lemon, rosewater and anis, dates back to the seventeenth century, and it has the great advantage of being very easy to make. I once put it on the menu at the British Embassy in Cairo and was pleased that it seemed to be very much to the taste of the sophisticated Cairenes invited to the luncheon.

You can, if you prefer, use dessert rather than cooking apples to make this tart, but will need 3 or 4 of them.

Roll out the pastry and cut 4 circles from it. Transfer them to a buttered and floured baking sheet and place three scented leaves on each round.

Peel, core and slice the apple, and arrange it on the

serves 4

250 g / ½ lb puff *or* sweet short pastry (p.66)

12 small rose geranium leaves (optional)

2 medium-sized Bramley or other tart cooking apples

2 tablespoons rosewater

4 tablespoons caster sugar

1 tablespoon fennel *or* anis seeds

grated zest of 1 lemon

25 g / 1 oz butter, softened

Taffety tart /continued

pastry. Brush with softened butter and then sprinkle on the fennel or anis seeds and lemon zest together with half the rosewater and sugar.

Bake for 15 to 20 minutes in an oven pre-heated to 180°C/350°F/gas mark 4. Remove from the oven and raise the heat to 200°C/400°F/gas mark 6. Brush the tarts with the remaining butter, scatter on the rest of the sugar and sprinkle them with the rest of the rosewater. Return the tarts to the oven and let them glaze and brown for 5 minutes.

Serve hot or warm, plain or with clotted cream, apple or rose petal sorbet, or vanilla ice-cream.

Rose and coconut macaroons

Coconut macaroons are an old-fashioned English tea-time treat, but so easy that a child could make them, under supervision. I added the rosewater flavour when I presented afternoon tea at the Mark Hotel in Manhattan. Early morning would find me baking trays and trays of macaroons, ready for the anglophile New Yorkers who came to enjoy scones and clotted cream, tea sandwiches, home-made ginger cake and petticoat tails. One teaspoon of rosewater should be sufficient, but you may need a little more, depending on its quality and strength.

makes about 20

125 g/4 oz desiccated coconut
125 g/4 oz icing sugar and rosewater to taste or
  125 g/4 oz rose petal sugar (p.29)
1 egg white
20 crystallised rose petals
rice paper

Mix the coconut and sugar, add a little rosewater and enough egg white to bind the mixture into a firm paste. Use teaspoons or dessertspoons, dipped in water, to shape small oval quenelles. Place them on a baking sheet lined with rice paper and bake for about 15 to 20 minutes in an oven pre-heated to 170°C/325°F/gas mark 3, until just pale gold. Remove from the oven, top each with a piece of crystallised rose petal and allow to cool on a wire rack. Small pieces of glacé cherries can be substituted for the rose petals.

Rose meringues

Put the egg white in a scrupulously clean bowl – even a slight trace of grease will prevent it attaining its full volume. Sprinkle on a tablespoon of sugar and begin whisking. When the egg white is foamy and increased in volume, add half the remaining sugar and continue whisking. The meringue will begin to take shape, becoming glossy and with smaller bubbles. Continue whisking until you have added all the sugar and the meringue is a firm mass of glossy foam with tiny bubbles. The mixture should peak and hold its shape when you trail the whisk through it.

Line a baking sheet with non-stick baking parchment or use a special baking mat. Spoon or pipe the meringue into four heaps and bake – or rather, dry – in an oven pre-heated to 125-150°C/250-300°F/gas mark 1 to 2 for about 45 minutes. Cool on a wire rack and store in an airtight tin until required.

makes 4

1 large egg white
100 g/scant 4 oz rose petal sugar
(p.29)

Cook's tip

For filled meringues, pipe or spoon into heaps on the baking sheet and, when cooked and cooled, sandwich with whipped cream flavoured with a splash of rosewater and, if you wish, delicately tinted with red food colouring.

Macarons à la rose

These are the authentic French *macarons* made with ground almonds. There are two factors essential to achieving success: the first is that the mixture must be glossy and smooth, with no bubbles from egg white that has been whisked too loosely, the second that the *macarons* must be allowed to dry out slightly before baking.

Sift the ground almonds and measured sugar together. This must be absolutely smooth and fine. Whisk the egg whites and, as they firm up, sprinkle in the powdered egg white and the additional tablespoon of icing sugar, together with the drop of food colouring – only a drop, mind – whisking until the mixture is very firm, smooth and glossy. Add some of the almond and sugar mixture to the egg white and fold in gently, and then gently fold in the remaining dry ingredients, which should finish with the consistency of soft paste and remain glossy and smooth.

Pipe into small mounds, about 2-3 cm/1 inch apart, on non-stick baking sheets. Let the *macarons* dry for about 20 minutes before baking them for 4 minutes at 150°C/300°F/gas mark 3. Turn the trays around and cook for another 4 minutes.

Allow to cool, then sandwich with rose petal jelly and rose butter cream.

makes about 40

125 g/generous 4 oz ground almonds
225 g/8 oz icing sugar, plus an additional tablespoon
1 tablespoon rose petal powder
100 ml/4 fl oz egg white (from 4 or 5 eggs)
a drop of red food colouring
1 teaspoon dried egg white (powder, optional)

Filling
rose petal jelly (p.170)
whipped cream or rose butter cream (see opposite)

Rose butter cream

Mix all the ingredients until you have a smooth mass. Store in an airtight container in the refrigerator.

makes approximately 500 g/1 lb

250 g/8 oz unsalted butter, softened but not oily
250 g/8 oz icing sugar
1 tablespoon rose petal powder
2 tablespoons rosewater
a dash of red food colouring

Rose sweetheart cake

A heart-shaped, rose-flavoured cake is exactly right for a special birthday tea or a St Valentine's Day treat.

Pre-heat the oven to 180°C/350°F/gas mark 4. Prepare a heart-shaped cake tin, or a round one if you prefer. Put half the sugar in a pudding basin and set it over a saucepan of hot water. Add the egg yolks and whisk until thick and pale. This will take about 5 minutes, during which time you should also whisk in the rosewater and food colouring. Whisk the egg whites with half the remaining sugar until peaks form. Fold in the last of the sugar and whisk until firm and glossy. Fold the sifted flour into the egg yolk mixture, and then add the egg white in the same way. Spoon into the tin, shaking so that it fills evenly. Bake for 10 to 12 minutes, until just firm to the touch. Turn out onto a cake rack and leave to cool.

Split horizontally and fill with whipped cream sweetened with the rose petal sugar. Just before serving, paint a heart in the middle of the cake with rose petal jelly and cover with fresh rose petals. Sift icing sugar over the border of the cake and serve.

serves 4–6

125 g/4 oz caster sugar
4 eggs, separated, plus an extra egg white
1 tablespoon rosewater
a dash of red food colouring
125 g/4 oz self-raising flour, sifted
200 ml/7 oz whipping cream
50 g/2 oz rose petal sugar, finely ground (p.29)
1 teaspoon rose petal jelly (p.170)
fresh or crystallised rose petals
icing sugar

Rose fairy cakes

Use a classic sponge mixture, rather than the flourless sponge above, to make dainty little cakes, sometimes called butterfly cakes, which were always known fairy cakes in our house when I was a child.

Cream the sugar and butter until pale and fluffy, then gradually add the whole egg and egg yolk, the rosewater, colouring and flour. Whisk the egg white until firm, fold into the cake mixture and spoon into well-buttered bun or muffin tins.

Bake in an oven pre-heated to 180°C/350°F/gas mark 4 for about 18 minutes, until well risen. Remove the cakes from their moulds and transfer them to wire racks to cool. Scoop a small, even round from the top of the cake and halve it. These two pieces will be the wings. Spoon a little rose butter cream into the hollow and balance the wings on top. Place in paper cases and dust lightly with icing sugar before serving.

makes 2 dozen

100 g/3 oz caster sugar
100 g/3 oz unsalted butter
2 eggs, 1 of them separated
1 tablespoon rosewater
a dash of red food colouring
125 g/4 oz self-raising flour, sifted

Flower fairy cakes

If you have plenty of time and patience, you can make a spectacular array of fairy cakes for a special occasion, such as a wedding or christening tea. Because of their sophisticated flavours, I don't think these would necessarily appeal to children. Rose and carnation fairy cakes, linden flower and elderflower fairy cakes, violet and lavender fairy cakes, marigold and nasturtium fairy cakes can all be created, using a delicate and sparing touch with the food colouring. For the last two, use shredded flowers in the cake batter and the butter cream. For the rest, you can use flavoured sugars, creams or pounded petals, whatever you find most convenient.

Coeurs à la crème

This is a very useful dessert, in that it positively demands to be made the day before it is eaten. The little French pierced porcelain moulds are something of an extravagance, as there is not much else one can use them for, but worth it; they should be lined with scalded muslin or cheesecloth. You can serve these cream cheese hearts throughout the summer and early autumn with a succession of different berries and fruits, fresh, poached or made into a coulis.

Blend the yoghurt and curd or cottage cheese and mix in the rosewater until smooth. Sweeten to taste and spoon the mixture into lined moulds, place on a plate and refrigerate for about 12 hours to drain and firm up.

When ready to serve, turn out onto plates and carefully peel the muslin from the pale creamy shape. Serve with a spoonful of rose petal jelly (p.170) and some poached cherries or lychees, both of which are delicious with any rose-flavoured accompaniment.

serves 6

250 ml/8 oz thick Greek-style plain yoghurt
150 g/5 oz curd cheese *or* sieved cottage cheese
2 teaspoons rosewater
rose petal sugar to taste (p.29)
3 egg whites

Rose petal jelly

This recipe produces a pale pinkish orange jelly, which is exquisite served with warm scones and clotted cream. Pure, but inexpensive, decadence. It also makes an instant dessert spooned over Greek yoghurt or ice-cream. Consider a rose vacherin for a most elegant note on which to finish a meal: a meringue on each plate, a layer of whipped cream, a quenelle of good ice-cream on top, a spoonful of rose petal jelly and a crystallised rose petal to finish it.

Wash and chop the apples, and put them – including both the skin and the cores – in a saucepan. Cover the apples by an inch or so of water and cook until the fruit is soft. Mash the fruit to extract as much juice and pectin as possible. Strain through a jelly bag for several hours or overnight.

Measure the volume of the jelly and then measure out an equal volume of sugar. Pound half the rose petals with a small amount of the sugar and mix with the juice and the rest of the sugar. Put in a preserving pan or heavy saucepan. Keep the rest of the petals to add later. Heat the saucepan gently and stir until the sugar has dissolved. Add the remaining rose petals and bring the syrup to boiling pint. Boil fast until setting point is reached and pot in small, clean, hot jam jars. Seal and label.

makes about 1 kg/2 lb

1 kg/generous 2 lb cooking
  apples
preserving sugar – see recipe
600 ml/1 pint dark red scented
  rose petals

Damask rose and black muscatel grape jelly

The juice of black grapes gives this jelly a sultry, dark red colour with an exquisite rose and muscatel flavour. The rose petals are best measured in a jug.

Wash and chop the apples and put them – including both the skin and the cores – in a saucepan and add enough water to cover them by an inch or so. Cook until the apple is almost soft, then add the stemmed grapes and cook until they too are soft. Mash the fruit to extract as much juice and pectin as possible and strain through a jelly bag for several hours or overnight.

Measure the liquid and then measure out an equal volume of sugar. Pound half the rose petals in a small quantity of the sugar and mix with the juice and the rest of the sugar. Put in a preserving pan or heavy saucepan. Keep the rest of the petals to add later. Gently heat the saucepan and cook until the sugar has dissolved. Add the remaining rose petals and bring the syrup to boiling pint. Taste and add the rosewater if you think it necessary. Boil fast until setting point is reached and pot in small, clean, hot jam jars. Seal and label.

makes about 1 kg/2 lb

1 or 2 large cooking apples
1 litre / 2 pints red grape juice
750 g–1 kg / 1½–2 lb black
    muscatel grapes
preserving sugar – see recipe
500–600 ml / about 1 pint or
    more dark red scented
    rose petals
1 tablespoon rosewater – if
    necessary

Rose sables

Use either of the rose petal jellies that precede this recipe as a filling for these traditional tea-time biscuits.

Use some of the butter to grease a baking sheet, then dust it lightly with flour. Put the rest of the flour, the sugar and the egg in a bowl or food-processor and mix for a few seconds, then add the butter and mix until a ball of dough is formed.

On a floured work-top, roll out the pastry to a little more than the thickness of a pound coin. Cut out 24 biscuits with a pastry cutter and then cut a hole out of the middle out of 12 of them. You might cut out heart-shaped biscuits, in which case use a smaller heart cutter for the centre. A fluted round biscuit can have a simple circle cut out of the middle. Diamonds, triangles and squares are also suitable shapes.

Place the biscuits on the baking sheet and bake for about 10 minutes in an oven pre-heated to 180°C/350°F/gas mark 4. When cooked, allow the biscuits to cool on a wire rack.

Spread the whole biscuits with rose petal jelly and thickly dust the remaining 12 with icing sugar. Put these on top of the jelly covered ones and spoon a little more jelly into the hole.

makes 20

250 g/8 oz unsalted butter, chilled
and diced
300 g/10 oz plain flour
100 g/4 oz granulated sugar
1 egg

To assemble
rose petal jelly (p.170)
icing sugar

Eton mess

This supremely easy dessert brings together the quintessential flavours of summer. Do not deprive yourself of this delicious flavour combination just because you have no rose petal jelly – simply use rosewater and sugar in place of the rose petal jelly.

Hull the strawberries and wipe both them and the raspberries. Put the fruit and jelly in a bowl and crush them with the back of a fork. Whip the cream and stir it and the crushed meringue into the fruit. Pile into glasses to serve.

serves 10

500 g / 1 lb strawberries
500 g / 1 lb raspberries
4 tablespoons rose petal jelly
   (p.170), or more to taste
600 ml / 1 pint whipping or double
   cream
4 or 5 broken meringue shells

Figs with rose petal jelly

The soft purple tenderness of September figs goes perfectly with the delicate scent and flavour of rose petals.

Trim the stalks from the figs and put them in a single layer in a shallow pan with the orange juice and zest. Cook gently until the figs are tender, turning them over if necessary. Add the jelly, cook for a minute or two more and transfer the figs to serving plates, with the cooking juices poured over. This is delicious served with yoghurt or clotted cream. I have occasionally served it with rose petal kulfi (p.176) for an extra dose of fragrance.

serves 4

8–12 figs
juice and finely pared zest of
   1 orange
4 tablespoons rose petal jelly
   (p.170)

Rose-baked peaches with zabaglione

This is a dish for a special occasion, ideally one on which you have some help with cooking or serving. It makes a perfect ending to a summer dinner, especially if all the preceding dishes were cold.

Peel the peaches, or not, as you prefer, and remove their stones by half slicing them. Butter a baking dish and place the peaches in it, dotting them with the rest of the butter. Then sprinkle on the rosewater, sugar and lemon juice. Bake the peaches at 180°C/350°F/ gas mark 4 until tender, which will take 30–40 minutes, basting them from time to time with the cooking juices.

To make the sauce, put the rose syrup, wine and egg in a bowl set over hot water. Use a whisk to lighten the sauce. Whisk until foamy and thick and serve with the baked peaches. Any cooking juices can also be whisked into the sauce. A crystallised rose petal might be used to decorate each serving.

serves 6

6 firm peaches
50 g / 2 oz unsalted butter, softened
1 tablespoon rosewater
1 tablespoon rose petal sugar (p.29)
1 tablespoon lemon juice
2 tablespoons rose syrup (p.32)
100 ml / 4 fl oz Moscato d'Asti or other unfortified sweet wine
2 large eggs

Rose-flavoured junket

Junket is a smooth, cool, milky pudding, something that you either love or loathe. I was never forced to eat it at school, so I see junket as a very agreeable ending to a summer meal, but there are people, who, recalling school meals, still shudder with horror if it is so much as mentioned.

In Anglo-Norman times junket was a soft, fresh cheese, so called for the *jonquet* or basket made from rushes (*jonques*) in which it was drained. And, indeed, making an unsweetened junket is still the first step to a home-made soft cheese. Once it has set, the solids are spooned into a sieve, colander or other pierced mould lined with a cheesecloth. The whey will drain off and the curds will be left behind to be pressed into a round or cylinder.

I like a simple, lightly sweetened junket best, with a sprinkling of nutmeg and a thin layer of cream poured on top when it has set. A tablespoon of brandy or rum might be stirred in with the sugar. When junket was more popular, cooks would ring the changes by flavouring it with rosewater, orange flower water or coffee.

Try it with a rose flavour and the merest hint of colouring, for an ethereal taste and texture. Use the best full-cream milk you can find, ideally Jersey or Guernsey.

Warm the milk and syrup to blood heat and no more. Remove from the heat and stir in the food colouring and rennet essence. Carefully pour into a bowl – glass for preference – and leave it at room temperature until the junket has set. After that, it can be refrigerated until required. If you like, run a layer of cream over the top before serving.

If you have them, you can cover the junket with a layer of rose petals, in shades of pink, just before serving.

serves 6

600 ml / 20 fl oz full-cream milk
2 tablespoons rose petal syrup
(p.32)
a spot of red food colouring
1 teaspoon rennet essence
150 ml / 5 fl oz whipping cream
(optional)

Rose petal kulfi

Cans of condensed and evaporated milk? Hardly the height of gastronomy, some might say, but do taste this heavenly ice-cream before you condemn it! This kulfi is ideal for those occasions when you need to be able to rustle up a quick dessert from the freezer. A recipe straight from the store-cupboard, this has an incomparable summer flavour and has the added advantage of not requiring an ice-cream machine.

Empty the contents of the cans and carton into a bowl, substituting a second can of evaporated milk for the cream if you would prefer the kulfi to be slightly less rich. Whisk well to combine the very different textures. Mix the melted rose petal jelly with the rosewater and powdered rose petals, then stir thoroughly into the milk mixture. Either pour into 8 dariole moulds or a shallow, rectangular container, so that you will get something about 4 cm/1^1/2 inches deep, and will be able to cut into 8 portions. Freeze for several hours, until thick but not hard. Break up the mixture and put it in the food-processor for a minute or so, processing until smooth, then refreeze until ready to use. Turn out, or cut up, and decorate each portion with a crystallised rose petal.

serves 8

1 x 400 ml/^{3}/4 pint tin sweetened condensed milk
1 x 400 ml/^{3}/4 pint tin evaporated milk
1 x 300 ml/^{2}/3 pint carton long-life cream
2 tablespoons rose petal jelly, melted
2 tablespoons rosewater
1 tablespoon powdered rose petals
a dash of cochineal or other red food colouring
8 crystallised rose petals

Rose cheesecake

This is a classic baked cheesecake, ideally served at room temperature on the day it is made. Avoid refrigerating it if you can, as doing so will soften the pastry.

Roll out the pastry and use it to line a cake tin, baking dish, flan ring or other suitable receptacle capable of holding a volume of about 600 ml/1 pint. Place the container on a baking sheet, as this will conduct heat right through the pastry, which has to hold a rather dense mixture.

To make the filling, first cream the cheese and sugar, then beat in the eggs and flour and finally the remaining ingredients. Pour into the pastry case and bake in an oven pre-heated to 180°C/350°F/gas mark 4 for between 45 minutes and 1 hour 15 minutes, depending on the depth of the filling. Keep the top pale, covering loosely with foil if it shows signs of browning.

Remove from the oven when a skewer inserted in the middle of the cake emerges clean. Allow the cheesecake to cool completely before decorating with rose petals and then slicing. If you have no rose petals, decorate the cheesecake with halved seedless red grapes and small bunches of the grapes that you have first 'frosted' by dipping them in whisked egg white and then icing or caster sugar.

For extra flavour and texture, you can add 50 g/2 oz ground almonds and two teaspoons of rose petal powder to the pastry, replacing an equal quantity of flour.

250 g/8 oz sweet short crust pastry (see p.66)

Filling
250 g/8 oz cream cheese or soft fresh cheese
50 g/2 oz caster sugar
25 g/1 oz rose petal sugar (p.29)
4 eggs
2 tablespoons plain flour, sifted
a drop of rose essence
2 tablespoons rosewater
juice of half a lemon
200 ml/7 oz single cream
150 ml/5 fl oz full-cream milk
crystallised or fresh rose petals for decoration

Chicken and almond pudding

Roses can be used in savoury as well as sweet dishes and go particularly well with chicken. In medieval times *blanc manger* – white dishes – of pounded almonds and chicken were flavoured with rosewater. I have developed something along similar lines that makes a perfect addition to a summer lunch. Your guests will be intrigued by the subtle flavour underlying the suave texture of the pounded chicken and almonds. The dish has something of the appearance of a *panna cotta* and looks very attractive when turned out of a pudding basin. It is best served warm or at room temperature, rather than hot, but is also good chilled.

Season the chicken breasts lightly with salt and white pepper and slightly more generously with mace. Remove any sinews and roughly chop the chicken. Then process it until you have a fine paste.

Gradually work in the cream until it is completely combined with the chicken. Stir in the almonds and rosewater and spoon into a lightly oiled pudding basin with a capacity of 1 litre/2 pints. Cover with cling film pierced in one or two places, then set on a trivet in a saucepan of simmering water or in a *bain-marie* and steam until the mixture is just firm. This should take about 40 to 50 minutes, but check after half an hour. The mixture is cooked when a knife-point or skewer inserted into the centre of the pudding emerges clean. Allow to cool for 10 minutes or so, then turn out onto a platter. Serve with a baby lettuce and rose petal salad dressed with rose petal vinegar (p.33) and extra virgin olive oil.

serves 6–8

3 skinless chicken breasts
white pepper
sea salt
½ teaspoon mace
450 ml/16 fl oz double cream
100 g/4 oz ground almonds
    sifted with
1 level tablespoon powdered rose
    petals
1 tablespoon rosewater

Cook's tip

To achieve a perfect, silky texture, you should rub the processed chicken through a sieve into a bowl set over ice cubes and mix the cream in with a wooden spoon. In addition, the almond ingredient should be almond milk, about 100 ml/4 oz, made by steeping 100 g/4 oz freshly skinned and ground almonds in 100 ml/4 fl oz hot water and squeezing through scalded muslin or cheesecloth.

Stuffed chicken breasts with roses and cucumber

This is a wonderfully summery dish, perfectly set off by the cucumber, which is all too often ignored as a vegetable suitable for cooking.

Shave the skin off the cucumber in thin strips and cut it in half lengthways. Scoop out and discard the seeds, then slice the cucumber as thinly as possible. Place the slices in a colander, sprinkle with salt and mix with your hands so that the cucumber is thoroughly salty. Leave to de-gorge over a bowl for an hour or so before rinsing thoroughly and drying with a clean tea-towel.

Remove the skin and any fat from the chicken breasts, as well as the arrow-shaped fillet underneath. Make a pocket in the chicken breasts with a sharp knife. Meanwhile prepare the stuffing.

Discard the sinew from the chicken fillets and trim any threads and green parts tainted by the gall bladder from the chicken livers. Roughly chop the liver and the fillet and blend them in a food-processor until smooth, then rub this mixture through a sieve. Blanch the rose petals in boiling water, refresh them under cold water, then dry them thoroughly and chop very finely. Mix the petals into the chicken stuffing, together with the cream and the seasoning. Spoon the mixture into the chicken breasts and secure with cocktail sticks.

Fry the chicken breasts in half the butter on both sides, cover partially and cook until the juices run clear. Place the chicken on a warm serving dish. Add the wine or stock and the rose vinegar to the pan juices, season lightly, scrape up any residues and add half the fresh rose petals. Cook for a minute or two and pour over the chicken.

Fry the cucumber in the remaining butter until wilted and bright green. Arrange it around the chicken and serve decorated with the rest of the rose petals.

serves 4

2 large cucumbers
1 tablespoon salt
4 chicken breasts, off the bone
25 g / 1 oz unsalted butter
2 tablespoons dry white wine *or* chicken stock
2 tablespoons rose petal vinegar (p.33)
salt
pepper
1–2 tablespoons fresh rose petals

Stuffing
2 chicken livers
4 chicken fillets
25 g / 1 oz rose petals
3 tablespoons double cream, clotted cream or crème fraîche
salt
pepper
nutmeg

Moroccan-style chicken pastries

Based on the famous *bistilla*, individual pastry parcels are here filled with a mixture of cooked chicken, eggs, dried fruit, rose-scented sugar and spices in an intriguing and subtle combination. Miniature versions make excellent hors d'oeuvres.

Beat the eggs with the stock and rosewater and cook gently in a non-stick frying pan, as if you were making scrambled eggs. When the mixture has thickened slightly, remove the pan from the heat and let it cool. Stir in the chicken and add the rest of the ingredients.

Stack up the pastry, brushing each sheet with melted butter. To make one parcel, take three squares, laying one on top of the other at an angle. Spoon some of the filling into the middle and dampen the pastry around the edges. Draw into the centre and enclose in a round parcel.

Place on a baking sheet, with the joins underneath, and bake for 20-25 minutes at 180°C/350°F/ gas mark 4. Serve hot, warm or cold, dusted with icing sugar and decorated with almonds, rose petals and mint leaves.

Cook's tip

If you have *ras el hanout*, use a tablespoon of it rather than the teaspoon each of cardamom, cumin and coriander.

Pickled lemons, an important ingredient in Moroccan cooking, are available in some specialist food shops. Alternatively, finely chop half a lemon, skin and all, and mix this, together with a generous pinch of salt, with the rest of the ingredients.

serves 6 to 8

750 g/1½ lb roasted, steamed or poached chicken, off the bone and finely chopped
6 eggs
150 ml/5 fl oz strong chicken stock
1 tablespoon rosewater
150 g/5 oz butter, melted
18 sheets of filo pastry or *feuille de brik*
75–100 g/3–4 oz rose petal sugar (p.29)
100 g/4 oz lightly toasted flaked almonds
1 teaspoon powdered cinnamon
150 g/5 oz chopped dried fruit, such as apricots, prunes, peaches or pears, or a mixture
50 g/2 oz pickled lemons, chopped (optional)
1 teaspoon cardamom, crushed
1 teaspoon cumin, crushed
1 teaspoon coriander seeds, crushed

Garnish
toasted almonds
rose petals
fresh mint leaves

Saffron

Nicholas Culpeper, who was apprenticed to the Apothecary of Cambridge University in the seventeenth century, wrote that saffron 'is a herb of the Sun, and under the Lion, and therefore you need not demand a reason why it strengthens the heart so exceedingly'. So I, born under the sign of Leo, need not look far to understand why saffron has long been one of my favourite flavourings. Moreover, unlike most of the flowers in this book, which are essentially summer food, saffron is available throughout the year and makes a heartening ingredient in winter soups and casseroles, the perfect antidote to chills and grey skies.

Saffron comes from the saffron crocus, *Crocus sativus*, which is not to be confused with *Colchicum autumnale*, the autumn crocus, sometimes referred to as meadow saffron, although nowadays it is more likely to be found as a garden plant than in the wild. Confusingly, both have bright pale purple flowers and bloom in the autumn, **but the autumn crocus is poisonous**.

Today, most of the saffron we buy comes from La Mancha in Spain, although it is also grown in Egypt, Greece, Iran, Kashmir and Morocco. A little is still grown in England, principally in Devon and Essex. In the Persian Gulf I used to buy exceptionally fine Iranian saffron, the stigmas arranged by hand in a flat, round box and tied in the shape of a peacock's tail. Unfortunately, it is very easy to imitate the

'Nor should I here omit saffron, which the German housewives have a way of forming into balls, by mingling it with a little honey; which thoroughly dried, they reduce to powder, and sprinkle it over their sallets for a noble cordial. Those of Spain and Italy, we know, generally make use of this flower, mingling its golden tincture with almost everything they eat.'

John Evelyn, *Acetaria*, 1699

appearance of dried saffron, although not its flavour, with the dried petals of the safflower, a member of the thistle family from which safflower oil is derived, so you should take care to buy this expensive ingredient from a reputable shop.

Saffron's slender red filaments, almost insignificant in themselves, add a rich colour, fragrance and inimitable flavour to food, qualities that were much prized throughout medieval Europe and are still highly valued today. Many a medieval banquet was enhanced by the use of saffron in 'gilding' food. Chickens, for example, were 'endored' with a saffron glaze before roasting. I have often done this with both chicken and turkey and it is most effective. Simply soak the saffron in a very little boiling water and paint it over the breast and legs of the bird about 20 minutes before cooking time is up.

Sadly, there is no evidence to support the legend that saffron was brought to Cornwall by the Phoenicians who came to trade for tin. Portugal is the furthest north they are thought to have reached, and there was plenty of tin to be had in the Iberian peninsula without the Phoenicians needing to brave the Bay of Biscay. Saffron was most probably introduced to Britain by the Romans and later brought back from the Middle East by pilgrims and Crusaders.

Saffron used to be harvested and sold at the great fair in Saffron Walden held every year on 21 October and at Newport Fair on 17 November. It has always been scarce and expensive and was a traditional gift from the Corporation of Saffron Walden to royal visitors to nearby Audley End in the sixteenth and seventeenth centuries.

At one time, saffron was used to tint butter and cheese a warm, appetising gold. Piacentinu, a Sicilian ewes' milk cheese made in Enna province, was first recorded in the fifteenth century and is still made today, still coloured and flavoured with saffron and black peppercorns, while the Umbrian cheese Fiore Molle is also subtly perfumed with saffron. Historically, saffron or carrot juice were used to colour English cheeses such as Red Leicester and Double Gloucester, a job nowadays done with annatto.

Shakespeare refers in *A Winter's Tale* to saffron as a colouring for warden pies, wardens being large, hard pears. Saffron cakes, buns and biscuits are still made in Devon, Cornwall, Northumberland and Ireland, especially at Easter time. At the wedding of my friend John Humphries, who used to import saffron, the cake had a glorious golden icing, coloured with saffron. He had also used saffron successfully, if somewhat expensively, to dye table linen, and wrote a fine book on the story of saffron and its many uses.

I use saffron a good deal in my cooking, and have included both savoury and sweet recipes in this chapter. Today we are accustomed to using saffron in dishes like risotto, paella and bouillabaisse, but there are also traditional English recipes for baked goods and desserts that employ saffron. One of the oldest I have come across, from the fourteenth-century recipe collection known as *The Forme of Cury* and first published in London in 1780, is an early version of cheesecake called *tart de Bry* (p.188) that uses honey, saffron and soft cheese mixed with eggs. I once served this at a gala dinner at the British Embassy in Paris, where I was invited to showcase English food and cooking. On other occasions, I have adapted it by using local ingredients – in Kuwait and Cairo, I made it with soft *labne*-type cheeses, and this was well received, perhaps because the result was not unlike some traditional Middle Eastern desserts.

Saffron works well with creamy desserts, but I advise against a saffron rice pudding. I have tried it several times, and although it tastes good, it looks too much like scrambled eggs, and has too similar a texture, for my eyes to tell my brain to tell my taste buds that it is indeed a delicious dessert.

I was first inspired to try my hand at saffron buns many years ago when talking to a friend who was brought up in Cornwall. I was delighted, when filming for television in the West Country, to be able to spend time in Warren's Bakery in St Just, as well as in private kitchens, watching the golden dough being prepared. Numerous recipes are to be found, some of which use the rubbing-in method, some the melted method. An Elizabethan version has the butter melted in sack or sherry, while Hannah Glasse offers the option of including caraway seeds, although she writes, 'I think it rather better without,' and I tend to agree with her. On the other hand, I like her suggestion of rosewater, another favourite English ingredient of the time, and one found in some of the many Cornish versions of saffron cake still in existence.

Saffron is costly: a one gram box contains about 540 filaments, the product of 180 hand-picked flowers. One-tenth of a gram, or about 50 filaments, is the amount required for many of the recipes that follow. Sachets of powdered saffron are available, weighing 0.1 or 0.125 grams, and one of these will colour and flavour a large loaf of bread, a paella for four people or the fish and saffron cassoulet on p.191.

Saffron buns

These buns are best served warm and freshly baked, perhaps best of all with 'thunder and lightning', in the Cornish manner, split and each half spread with clotted cream, over which you trickle some treacle.

Sprinkle the dried yeast on 150 ml/5 fl oz of the milk, together with 1 teaspoon of sugar, and let it work for 10 to 15 minutes. Meanwhile, soak the saffron in 2 to 3 tablespoons of very hot water. Rub the fat into the flour, stir in the sugar, fruit and the mixed peel. Make a well in the centre and pour in the yeast mixture, the rosewater – if using it – and the saffron liquid. Combine to a dough, adding more warm milk as necessary. Knead on a floured work-top until smooth and place in an oiled bowl. Cover with a clean, damp tea-towel and let the dough rise for an hour or so in a draught-free place.

makes about 2 dozen

1 tablespoon fast action
    dried yeast
up to 450ml/16 fl oz warm milk
100 g/4 oz caster sugar
1/10 g/50 saffron filaments or
    1 sachet powdered saffron
250 g/8 oz butter or lard, or a
    mixture of the two
750 g/1½ lb strong, plain flour
250 g/8 oz seedless raisins
    or sultanas
50–75 g/2–3 oz mixed candied
    peel
1–2 tablespoons rosewater
    (optional)

Knock the dough back and shape into buns. Put these on a non-stick baking sheet, cover again and let them rise for a further 30 to 40 minutes. Bake for 40 to 50 minutes in an oven pre-heated to 180°C/350°F/gas mark 4. If you wish, the buns can be brushed with an egg and milk glaze before baking.

Saffron ciabatta

I first developed this recipe when teaching a cookery course in Andalusia, where saffron is more widely used than in Italy, home of the ciabatta.

Infuse the saffron in a little of the water. Briefly spin the flour and yeast together with the dough-blade attachment of the food-processor. Then, with the motor on, add the oil, salt and enough water, including all the saffron water, to make a firm batter or loose dough. The texture is right when it is sticky but not wet, and adheres to itself rather than your hands. Process for a minute, scraping the dough from the sides. You can then put the feed tube in the lid to provide a seal and leave the dough for at least 3 hours, preferably 6 or longer. I have done it this way, and it works satisfactorily, but I prefer to wash the food-processor bowl and get it out of the way, so I scrape the dough into a large bowl, which I first warm with hot water to prevent it from cooling down too rapidly.

Cover with oiled cling film, or put inside a large, oiled polythene bag, which should be tightly closed. Once the dough is ready, have a non-stick baking sheet or Swiss roll tray ready and gently ease the dough onto it with a rolling motion. Flouring the hands first helps. Dust the top with flour and leave to prove for 30 to 40 minutes. The dough will not rise much at this stage but just plump out a little. Pre-heat the oven to 220°C/425°F/gas mark 7 and bake for about 30 minutes until the loaf is golden brown and hollow-sounding. The bread will puff up considerably in baking.

makes one 20 cm/8 inch loaf

$1/20$ g/25 saffron filaments or
    $1/2$ sachet powdered saffron
250 g/8 oz strong plain flour
$1/2$ teaspoon fast action dried yeast
5 tablespoons extra virgin olive oil
$1/2$ teaspoon salt
about 200 ml/7 fl oz hand-hot
    water

Quick saffron bread

Using fast action yeast, this dough requires only one rising and produces an excellent all-purpose bread, good with salted butter and honey for tea or to accompany a cheese board or a slice of terrine.

Put the saffron in a bowl and pour on a little of the boiling water. Mix the dry ingredients in a bowl or food-processor and then add the olive oil, saffron liquid and the rest of the water, which should be stirred together. When the dough is thoroughly mixed, knead it for 10 minutes on a floured surface until smooth and elastic. Divide and shape as appropriate and place in greased tins or, if you are making bread rolls, a cottage loaf or a plait, onto a non-stick baking sheet. Cover with a damp tea-towel and leave to rise until doubled in volume. Bake in an oven pre-heated to 230°C/450°F/gas mark 8 for about 35 to 40 minutes for a large loaf, 30 minutes for 2 small loaves or 15 to 20 minutes for bread rolls.

makes one 1 kg / 2 lb loaf or
two smaller loaves

$1/10$ g / 50 saffron filaments or
1 sachet powdered saffron
150 ml / 5 fl oz boiling water
750 g / 1½ lb strong white flour
2 teaspoons salt
1 teaspoon fast action dried yeast
4 tablespoons extra virgin olive oil
300 ml / ½ pint cold water

Fried saffron bread

This rich and delightful version of French toast, or the Spanish *torrijas*, is a perfect quick pudding. I used cider to make it when I was in the West Country, but you can substitute dessert wine or sherry as the mood takes you.

Beat the egg and cider in a shallow basin and dip the saffron bread in it, making sure the bread is well coated on both sides. Fry in the butter until crisp and serve hot with a dollop of cold clotted cream and some honey.

serves 2 to 4

1 egg
150 ml / 5 fl oz dry cider
4 slices saffron bread
50 g / 2 oz unsalted butter

to serve
honey and clotted cream

Saffron bread and butter pudding

You can make this with bought saffron cake, sliced saffron buns or quick saffron bread (see the previous recipe). If you use the latter, you might want to sprinkle a handful of raisins or sultanas and some chopped mixed peel between the layers of buttered bread.

Generously butter an oven-proof dish and lay the pieces of bread in it. Beat the eggs, milk and cream, pour over the bread and leave it to stand for 20 minutes or so before baking for 35 to 40 minutes in an oven pre-heated to 180°C/350° F/gas mark 4.

serves 8 to 10

25 g/1 oz butter
sliced saffron bread, liberally
    buttered and cut into triangles
4 eggs
300 ml/½ pint full-cream milk
300 ml/½ pint single cream

Saffron and honey custards

These offer a pleasing alternative to crème caramel and can also be served as part of a trio of flavoured custards, perhaps chocolate, vanilla and saffron.

Put the cream into a saucepan with the saffron and, while you bring it to the boil, lightly beat together the sugar and eggs. Pour the boiling cream over the beaten eggs and sugar, stirring continuously. Put 4 or 6 ramekin dishes in a roasting tin with enough water to come half-way up their sides. Pour the mixture into the ramekins, cover with foil and bake in the middle of an oven pre-heated to 160°C/325°F/gas mark 3 for about 30 minutes, or until a knife-point inserted in the middle comes out clean.

Cool and then refrigerate for 2 to 3 hours, or overnight. To serve, run a little clear honey over the custards and, if you wish, scatter on some flaked almonds.

serves 4 to 6

600 ml/1 pint single or
    double cream
1/20 g/25 saffron filaments or
    ½ sachet powdered saffron
1 tablespoon caster sugar
4 eggs

Saffron, cheese and honey tart

This is my version of the medieval *tart de Bry* mentioned in the introduction to this chapter. When serving it on a truly special occasion, I sometimes use a little gold leaf to decorate the top. It is best made with a soft, mild Brie.

Start by blind-baking either a plain or a sweet short crust flan case following the instructions on p.66. Use a 25 cm/10 inch rimmed pie plate, using the trimmings to decorate the rim with pastry leaves or, if you prefer, a plait. When it is cooked, remove from the oven, take out the beans and paper and allow the pastry case to cool. Meanwhile, soak the saffron for 20 minutes in a tablespoon of hot water.

Put the Brie in a bowl and mix it thoroughly with the cream cheese. Melt the honey with the milk, stir in the saffron liquid and the cheese and beat in the eggs. Pour the mixture carefully into the pie dish and bake in an oven pre-heated to 190°C/375°F/gas mark 5 for 15 minutes, then reduce the heat to 170°C/325°F/ gas mark 3 for a further 20 minutes or so. Serve warm or cold, dusted with a little icing sugar, perhaps with clotted cream.

serves 4 to 6

$\frac{1}{10}$ g/50 saffron filaments or
   1 sachet powdered saffron
1 short crust or sweet short crust
   flan case, baked blind –
   see p.66
250 g/8 oz Brie, rind removed
250 g/8 oz cream or curd cheese
3 tablespoons honey
4–5 tablespoons milk
3 eggs

Cook's tip

If you prefer a simple saffron and honey cheesecake, you can use all cream cheese or curd cheese in place of the Brie. I have also made a 'cheesecake' with Greek yoghurt, which I have strained for a few hours, thereby further reducing the moisture content.

Saffron and honey junket

A honey-sweetened saffron junket makes an unusual ending to a meal, the junket traditional, the flavourings modern in application. Honey really is the perfect sweetener for saffron-flavoured desserts, whether creams, custards, pies or cakes. It goes almost without saying that junket is not worth making unless you use good quality, fresh, creamy milk. Those lucky enough to have access to raw milk will be able to make a good junket. Otherwise, look for gold top, the Guernsey or Jersey milk that has at least 5 per cent fat. Junket is best made in a glass bowl.

Warm the saffron liquid, milk and honey to blood heat, but no more, then remove from the stove and stir in the rennet essence. Carefully pour into a bowl and leave it at room temperature until the junket has set. After that, it can be refrigerated until required. If you like, you can run a layer of cream over the top before serving.

serves 4 to 6

$1/10$ g / 50 saffron filaments or
   1 sachet powdered saffron,
   soaked in 2 tablespoons
   boiling water
600 ml / 1 pint full-cream milk
1 tablespoon honey
1 teaspoon rennet essence
150 ml / 5 fl oz whipping cream
   (optional)

Albi

A few years ago I revisited Albi, where I had earlier
spent a very happy year as an *assistante* at the town's
Ecole Normale. On my return trip I investigated the
food of the Tarn and was surprised at the use of
saffron, which I had never particularly associated with
French cooking. Five hundred years ago this part of
Languedoc was famous for its woad production,
supplying much of renaissance Europe with high-
quality blue dye. This crop was later replaced by
saffron, which became an important ingredient in
many of the region's dishes.

Tripe in saffron sauce

This is a version of *gras double à l'albigeoise*, which
never works quite as well in England, where tripe is
bleached and processed almost beyond recognition.

Bring half the wine to the boil, pour it onto the
saffron and leave to infuse while you prepare the rest
of the recipe. Heat half the fat or oil and gently fry the
onions and ham in it for 5 minutes. Sprinkle on the
flour and stir it in, cooking until the flour just begins
to turn colour, and then add the cloves. Gradually add
the saffron-scented wine, the stock and the rest of the
wine, stirring continuously to prevent lumps from
forming. Cook the roux gently while you prepare the
tripe as follows.

Dry the tripe very thoroughly, but you will be
surprised at how much liquid is released when you fry
it in the remaining fat. Discard as much of this liquid
as you can, or cook the tripe long enough for the
liquid to evaporate. Add the garlic, parsley and saffron
liquid to the roux, stir it in with the tripe and cook
together for 10 minutes or so.

Season and serve from a heated earthenware dish or
casserole. Steamed or boiled potatoes go well with it.

serves 4

300 ml/½ pint dry white wine
1/10 g/50 saffron filaments or
    1 sachet powdered saffron
2 tablespoons duck fat or
    sunflower oil
2 onions, sliced
100 g/4 oz ham or bacon, diced
2 tablespoons flour
2 or 3 cloves
300 ml/½ pint beef, veal or
    chicken stock
2 kg/4 lb ox tripe
4 cloves garlic, crushed
2 tablespoons parsley, finely
    chopped
salt
pepper

Fish and saffron cassoulet

Inspiration from the same part of France is also responsible for this recipe, which I devised on my return home from Albi. If you forget to soak the cannellini overnight, you can use a couple of 400g/ 14 oz cans of white beans.

Fry the bacon or pork briefly in the duck fat or olive oil and then add the onions and garlic. Cook without browning for a few minutes, then add the rest of the ingredients, except the fish and the breadcrumbs. Bring to the boil, partially cover and simmer until the beans are tender. If you are using canned beans, do not add them until the mixture has simmered long enough to cook the bacon and onion. Rub a few beans through a sieve to thicken the mixture.

Cut the fish into chunks, stir into the beans, scatter breadcrumbs on the surface of the pot and finish off, uncovered, for 15 to 20 minutes in an oven pre-heated to 200°C/400°F/gas mark 6. Serve with chopped parsley on top.

serves 6

4–6 rashers streaky bacon or
   100 g/4 oz salt pork, diced
1 tablespoon duck fat or extra
   virgin olive oil
2 onions, thinly sliced
6 cloves garlic, crushed
2 tablespoons parsley, finely
   chopped, plus extra for garnish
$^1/_{10}$ g/50 saffron filaments or
   1 sachet powdered saffron
300 ml/½ pint dry white wine
750 g/1½ lb fish, prepared
   weight (see Cook's tip below)
400 g/14 oz cannellini or other
   white beans, soaked overnight
   and par-boiled
600 ml/1 pint fish stock
4 tablespoons breadcrumbs

Cook's tip

Salmon, cod, salt cod (which needs to be soaked in fresh water for 48 hours before cooking) and some shellfish make a very good combination of fish. Cod, haddock or monkfish and mussels would also work well.

Cornwall

While working in the West Country, I developed a number of useful recipes featuring saffron, fish – both fresh and smoked – and shellfish.

Mussels in cider and saffron

This tasty dish is based on *moules marinière*, with cider replacing the white wine.

Scrub the mussels well under cold running water and remove their beards and any barnacles, discarding any open (dead) mussels. Put the vegetables, pepper, saffron and cider in a heavy-lidded casserole, bring to the boil, cover and simmer for a few minutes until the vegetables are tender. Open the casserole, tip in the well-rinsed mussels, replace the lid and give the casserole a vigorous shake in order to distribute the vegetables and seasoning.

Let the mussels steam for 5 minutes or so. Serve from the pot with bread to mop up the juices. A dollop of clotted cream can be added to enrich the sauce.

serves 2 as a main course,
4 as a starter

2 kg / 4 lb mussels
1 small onion, finely chopped
2 celery stalks, finely sliced
1 leek, thinly sliced
1 carrot, grated
1/2 teaspoon pepper
300 ml / 1/2 pint dry cider
1/20 g / 25 saffron filaments
  pounded in a mortar or
  1/2 sachet powdered saffron

Mussel and saffron griddle cakes

This is not a traditional recipe, but simply a combination of two wonderfully complementary flavours that I like to serve with a glass of well-chilled *fino* or Chablis.

Start by lightly steaming the well scrubbed mussels and, when they are cool enough to handle, remove them from their shells.

Beat the saffron water, flour, egg and buttermilk to form a thick batter. Heat the pan and, just before you are ready to cook, sprinkle the baking powder into the batter and beat it again thoroughly. Then stir in the mussels, seasoning and snipped up herbs.

Pour a small ladle of batter into the pan. Do not shake the pan to spread the mixture. These will be small, quite thick cakes. You will probably be able to cook four at a time. When the top surface looks matt and full of holes, flip the cakes over to cook the underside for 2 to 3 minutes. Serve either hot or warm.

makes 12 to 16

1 kg / 2 lb mussels
$1/20$ g / 25 saffron filaments or
  $1/2$ sachet powdered saffron,
  soaked in hot water
100 g / 4 oz plain flour
1 egg
150 ml / 5 fl oz buttermilk or
  yoghurt thinned down with water
2 scant teaspoons baking powder
chives, chervil or parsley
oil or butter for frying
salt
pepper

Cook's tip

Clams, cockles, whitebait, oysters or queen scallops can replace the mussels.

Golden fish chowder

This warming fish soup, which is substantial enough to serve as a main course, is given a beautiful golden colour and warm spiciness by the saffron. Do not be tempted to use dyed smoked haddock – naturally smoked, un-dyed fish has an infinitely superior flavour and texture. You can use the skin from the fish fillets to make the fish stock, together with any trimmings removed from the bones, and can also, of course, ask your fishmonger for some extra fish bones for stock.

Heat the oil or butter in a large saucepan or casserole and gently cook the onion and potatoes, without browning, until the onion is translucent. Pour on the fish stock, add the saffron, coriander or dill stalks and bay leaf, and simmer until the potatoes are soft. Remove the herbs.

If you want a thicker soup, at this stage you can mash some of the potato into the soup. Skin the fish fillets, cut them into chunks and add them to the soup. Barely simmer for 2 to 3 minutes, until the fish is just cooked through. Season to taste with pepper and – if using them – stir in chopped fresh coriander or dill.

serves 6

2 tablespoons extra virgin olive oil or butter
1 onion, chopped
500 g / 1 lb potatoes, diced
1 litre / 2 pints fish stock
$1/20$ g / 25 saffron filaments or $1/2$ sachet powdered saffron, soaked in hot water
a handful of fresh coriander or dill (optional)
1 bay leaf
500 g / 1 lb un-dyed smoked haddock fillet
250 g / $1/2$ lb fresh haddock fillet
pepper

Cornish crab and saffron soup

This is based on a recipe I cooked when I was in the West Country, and I have further developed it to include saffron, which serves as a nice counterpoint to the crab's natural sweetness.

Place the rice, milk, saffron and butter in a pan with salt, pepper and nutmeg to taste. Bring to the boil and simmer until the rice is tender. Add the brown crab meat, setting aside the white meat from the claws. Rub the mixture through a sieve or blend it in a liquidiser, then return it to the pan and add the stock, anchovy essence and white crab meat. Adjust the seasoning and stir in the cream. Heat the soup through without allowing it to boil.

serves 6

1 large cooked crab, weighing
    about 1–1.5 kg / 2–3 lb
75 g / 3 oz long grain rice
1 litre / 2 pints milk
1/10 g / 50 saffron filaments or
    1 sachet powdered saffron
25g / 1 oz butter
nutmeg
1 litre / 2 pints chicken stock, or
    stock made from the crab shell
    and claw-ends
1 teaspoon anchovy essence
150 ml / 5 fl oz single cream
salt
pepper

Smoked haddock salad with oysters in saffron and cider vinaigrette

When I cooked a West Country dinner at London's Groucho Club, I wanted to use typical ingredients in a cold first course and this is what I came up with. The quantities given here are generous, as this makes a very good winter buffet dish.

Start by poaching the fish very lightly in the cider with the saffron, keeping a few filaments to one side, and mustard. Remove the fish and boil the liquor until it is reduced by about a half. Add the herbs, the remaining saffron, just a dash of cider vinegar and plenty of olive oil to make a vinaigrette. Put the salad leaves on plates or a large platter and the fish on top with the leeks around it. Place a poached oyster on top of each portion of fish and spoon on the dressing.

The leeks, whatever their size, should be trimmed, cut into narrow strips, well washed and drained, and then steamed. To poach the oysters, first shuck them, retaining as much of their liquid as possible but discarding any pieces of shattered shell. Put the oysters and their liquid in a saucepan and heat gently until the liquid just starts to tremble. Remove from the heat and leave the oysters in their liquid before scooping out with a slotted spoon.

serves 10

1.5 kg / 3 lb *un-dyed* smoked haddock, filleted, skinned and portioned
600 ml / 1 pint dry cider
¹⁄₁₀ g / 50 saffron filaments or 1 sachet powdered saffron
2 tablespoons grain mustard
2 tablespoons each chopped chives and parsley
a dash of cider vinegar
extra virgin olive oil
salad leaves
10 rock oysters, poached – see recipe
1 kg / 2 lb large or 30 baby leeks – see recipe
salt
pepper

Mousseline of scallop roe with saffron sauce

I am particularly fond of this recipe, which I developed more than 20 years ago, as it contributed to my winning the cookery competition that was the start of my career as a chef and food writer.

Pre-heat the oven to 150°C/300°F/gas mark 2; if your oven is on the hot side, use a slightly lower setting. Rinse the scallops free of sand and remove the thick pad of muscle and the roe or coral. Set aside 6 or 8 of the best-shaped scallops – these you can sauté and serve with the mousselines. Put the rest of the scallops, their roes, eggs, half the cream and a little seasoning in a food-processor, blend until smooth and then sieve.

Butter 6 small ramekins or decorative bavarois moulds and set them in a roasting tin containing a little water. Fill the ramekins almost to the top with the scallop mixture, place them in the middle of the oven and cook for 25 minutes. The exact cooking time will depend on the depth of the mixture; a knife-point inserted in the centre will come out clean when the mousseline is cooked.

To prepare the sauce, fry the shallot in half the butter until it is soft but not brown. Add the fish stock and boil to reduce by a third. Stir in the saffron and remaining cream and cook for 5 minutes. Strain and keep the sauce warm. Turn the mousselines out onto heated individual serving plates, mop up any liquid with a paper towel and surround each with a few spoonfuls of sauce and some toasted nuts.

serves 6

10–12 scallops with large roes
3 eggs
150 ml/5 oz double cream
1 shallot, finely chopped
75 g/3 oz unsalted butter
425 ml/15 fl oz fish stock
$1/20$ g/25 saffron filaments or
    $1/2$ sachet powdered saffron,
    steeped in 2 tablespoons
    hot water
salt
white pepper

Garnish
toasted flaked almonds or
    pine kernels

Spain

Introduced by the Moors, who also brought rice to the Iberian peninsula, saffron has long played an important part in Spanish cooking. I remember travelling one autumn day by train to Toledo and seeing a field of saffron crocus in full bloom – I was crossing the La Mancha plain, the world's largest saffron-producing area. Over the course of many visits to Spain, I have learnt to cook a variety of savoury dishes flavoured with saffron, which has a particular affinity with both rice and fish.

Tuna with onion, *fino* and saffron

One of my favourite Spanish restaurants is the Bar Bigote in Sanlúcar de Barrameda, downstream from Seville at the mouth of the Guadalquivir, run by the Hermoso brothers. Here is one of their excellent fish recipes – you will find that it also works very well with thick cod or even salmon fillets.

Cut the fish into 5 cm/2 inch chunks, season lightly and put to one side while you cook the onion in olive oil. This will take 40 to 50 minutes, as the onion should be cooked almost to a purée by the time you add the fish, which will only take a few minutes to cook. Bring the *fino* to the boil, pour it over the saffron and leave to soak. When the onion is soft, add the fish and the saffron-scented *fino*, bring to just below simmering point, cover and cook very gently for 3 to 4 minutes. Transfer the fish to heated plates or a serving dish and boil up the sauce. If you are using peas, add them at this stage. Cook for a minute or two more and then spoon the sauce over the fish. A bowl of rice or some boiled potatoes are the perfect accompaniment for this fish stew.

serves 4–6

750 g/1½ lb tuna fillet
freshly ground black pepper
1 large mild onion, sliced
2–3 tablespoons extra virgin
    olive oil
$\frac{1}{10}$ g/50 saffron filaments or
    1 sachet powdered saffron
150 ml/5 fl oz *fino* (dry sherry)
a handful or two of fresh or frozen
    peas (optional)
sea salt

Paella with rabbit and snails

A Valencian cook taught me this recipe and, although I have had delicious seafood paellas in Alicante, it remains my favourite. Some of the earliest known recipes for paella involve rabbit and snails, so this is a dish with a sound historical pedigree. Bomba, Calasparra or Valencia are the rice varieties with which to make paella; they can be found in the specialist sections of larger supermarkets as well as in delicatessens and Spanish food shops.

Soak the saffron threads in 1/4 teacup of hot water. Then fry the rabbit pieces in the olive oil until golden brown in a heavy frying pan, casserole or paella pan. Stir in the rice to coat it with oil and then add the vegetables. Pour on the saffron liquid and about a quarter of the stock; stir in and let it cook gently, if possible with a heat-diffuser between the pan and the heat.

As the liquid evaporates, add a little more, stirring, and repeat this process until all the vegetables are tender. Add the prepared snails after about 20 minutes. Season lightly, then cover tightly with a lid or foil and let the paella stand in a warm place for 10 minutes. The rice will continue to swell and cook. The resulting dish should be neither dry nor soupy, but moist. If you prefer, chicken can be used instead of rabbit.

serves 4 to 6

1/20 g / 25 saffron filaments or
    1/2 sachet powdered saffron
1.5 kg / 3 lb rabbit portions, cut
    into 12 pieces
5 tablespoons extra virgin olive oil
400 g / 14 oz paella rice
4 cloves garlic, finely chopped
250 g / 8 oz asparagus, cut into
    2.5 cm / 1 inch pieces
250 g / 8 oz green beans
    (shelled weight)
250 g / 8 oz broad beans
    (shelled weight)
2 tomatoes, peeled, seeded and
    chopped
1 litre / 2 pints vegetable *or*
    chicken stock or water and dry
    white wine mixed
1 can snails, rinsed and drained
salt
pepper

Calasparra rice and beans with red peppers

This is an unusual rice dish I discovered when I visited Calasparra, near Murcia, where the very best Spanish rice is grown.

Soak the beans overnight and simmer them until tender the following day, reserving the liquid in which they cook.

About 45 minutes before you plan to serve the rice, heat the oil in a paella pan and gently fry the spring onions, garlic and crushed pimentos for a few minutes. Remove and put to one side.

Fry the tomato, and then add the rice, the rest of the ingredients, and 3 times as much water as rice, including the liquid in which the beans were cooked. Bring to the boil, add the beans and cook for about 20 minutes. Serve immediately.

serves 4–6

200 g / 7oz dried large white beans, or butter beans, or the smaller cannellini, or haricot beans
3 tablespoons olive oil
3 cloves garlic, chopped
6 spring onions, trimmed and chopped
2 dried red pimentos
2 tomatoes, peeled, seeded and chopped
300 g / 10 oz Calasparra rice
1/2 teaspoon salt
1/10 g / 50 filaments or
    1 sachet powdered saffron
2 tablespoons chopped parsley
water

Violets and pansies

When I was a small child living in the country, violets grew wild along our garden path and I would pick them to serve for my dolls' tea parties. Later, having moved to the city, I would buy them from a stall in Leeds Market, wrapped in cool green ivy leaves, but I'm afraid I wouldn't be quite as trusting of violets bought today, as there are worrying stories of them being drenched in artificial scent before being put on sale. Nowadays, sadly, you need to grow your own violets in order to have sufficient flowers for cooking.

Much later, when I lived in the Languedoc, trips to Toulouse always included a visit to one of the city's many *confiseries* specialising in *violettes de Toulouse*, crystallised violets, wonderful chocolates filled with violet cream and other delicacies made from this very special flower. In 2004 the city hosted the International Violet Meeting, at which violet growers and aficionados from all over the world came together to listen to experts, visit violet growers in the surrounding countryside and to feast on violet-flavoured dishes.

'I do not know which pleased grandma best, when we carried her home a lapful of eggs, or a few violets: for she was particularly fond of violets.'

Charles Lamb, *Essays of Elia*

Warning

Despite their name, colour and appearance, African Violets or St Paulia are not members of the viola family and are not edible.

Violet cream

Dorothy Hartley describes a fourteenth-century recipe for a violet sweet, a pottage, in which the flowers are pounded with almonds, ground rice and sugar then boiled in milk. It is not unlike a flavoured ground rice pudding, and led me to experiment with rice milk and rice flour. These are very delicately flavoured ingredients, particularly suitable for subtle flower flavours and an excellent alternative if you do not want to use milk, cream or almonds.

serves 4

2 tablespoons granulated sugar
a generous handful of violets,
    green parts removed
2 tablespoons rice flour
300 ml / ½ pint rice milk
a drop of violet essence (optional)
a drop of food colouring (optional)

Put the sugar and flowers in a mortar and pound them to a paste. Mix the rice flour with a little of the rice milk in a saucepan, then gradually stir in the rest of the ingredients until you have a thin cream. Gently bring to the boil, stirring continuously to smooth out any lumps, cook for 3 or 4 minutes – you will notice the mixture thickening – stir in the flower paste and the essence and colouring, if using them. Mix well and pour into custard cups or glasses. Allow to cool and then chill until required. You can garnish with frosted fresh flowers or crystallised flowers – see p.36.

Cook's tip

This is a good blueprint for other flower 'creams' if you wish to avoid dairy products. It is particularly good made with roses.

Summer fruit sundae with violet syrup

Soft berry fruits match the delicate floweriness of
violets, or you might try using pale-fleshed melons,
piel de sapo or honeydew rather than canteloup.
Needless to say, you should use the best ice-cream you
can find or afford when making this delicious dessert.

Prepare the fruit and divide it amongst six glass bowls.
Place a scoop of ice-cream on top, spoon over the
syrup and top with a crystallised violet.

If you use the commercial violet syrup, I suggest
diluting it in plain sugar syrup, otherwise the colour
will be too dark and dense, and the flavour will also be
very strong.

serves 6

1 punnet each of raspberries,
   strawberries and blueberries
6 scoops vanilla ice-cream
6 dessert spoons home-made
   violet syrup (p.32)
6 crystallised violets

Violet Turkish delight

This method can be adapted to any of the scented
flowers that feature in this book, and for a very special
occasion you might even want to make up a batch
scented with rose, elderflower, jasmine, lavender and
violet. Naturally, you can only make this in summer,
but Turkish delight keeps well in a dark, cool and,
above all, dry place, so you will be able to offer unique
gifts at Christmas, prettily packaged in glass bowls or
lined baskets covered with cellophane.

This is one recipe in which I will happily use food
colouring, albeit very sparingly. Sweets are meant to
be colourful.

Start with a violet syrup, or any flower syrup, using
the method described on p.32, but making double the
quantity and without adding lemon juice. If using
lavender, you will need much less, as they are far more
strongly scented, so 5–10 g/1–2 teaspoons lavender
flowers will be sufficient for 1.2 kg/2 lb 10 oz sugar.

Remove all the green parts from the flowers, put

makes about 750 g/1½ lb

100 g/4 oz violet flowers
600 ml/20 fl oz boiling water
1.2 kg/2 lb 10 oz granulated
   sugar
¼ teaspoon tartaric acid
225 g/7 oz cornflour (cornstarch)
a dash of violet essence (optional)
purple food colouring (optional)
icing sugar

Violet Turkish delight /continued

them in a non-reactive saucepan and pour on the boiling water. Stir in the sugar until dissolved, add the tartaric acid, bring back to the boil and simmer for 1 minute. Remove from the heat and infuse overnight.

Next day, smear a square cake tin with an oil like grapeseed that will not flavour the sweet. Then mix 125 g/4 oz of the cornflour with about 30 ml/2 fl oz of water in a large saucepan, strain the syrup into the pan and stir the mixtures together.

Bring to the boil and cook to the 'soft ball' stage, that is 112–116°C/230–240°F on a sugar thermometer. To test this without a thermometer, drop a little of the mixture into a bowl of cold water and work it with your fingers. It should be pliable and hold together. It will have reached this stage once you have cooked the mixture until it begins to leave the side of the pan.

Put the remaining cornflour on one half of the work surface – a marble top is ideal – and the icing sugar on the other. Turn the Turkish delight first on to the cornflour, both sides, then dust off any excess. Use a sharp knife to cut the sweet into squares, coat the pieces well in icing sugar and store in an airtight container between layers of waxed paper.

Violet jelly

Using apple and red grapes as the base, *sirop de violettes* from Toulouse and a dash of violet essence (see p.44) makes a very good jelly. You need to rely on your palate and eye to judge quantities, as the colour will depend on how much colour the grape skins release as you cook them. Spooned over ice-cream on top of a meringue, the jelly makes an exquisite dessert. I also use it as the base for my violet ice-cream.

Chop up the apple and put it with its skin and core in a saucepan with the grapes. Remove the latter from the main stem, but there is no need to de-stalk them, as everything will be strained through a jelly bag.

Just cover the fruit with water, add the lemon juice and cook until the fruit is soft. Crush with a potato masher. Wet a jelly bag, suspend it over a wide-mouthed container and spoon the fruit pulp into the bag. Let it drip until the pulp has no more to yield, although you can help it along with a gentle squeeze as long as none of the pulp seeps through. Then carefully add the violet syrup to give the hint of blue that will turn the juice to a thrilling violet shade.

Measure the volume of the liquid. It will probably be about 500 ml/18 fl oz. Measure out an equivalent amount of sugar – 500 g/18 oz – and put both it and the juice in a large saucepan. Bring to the boil slowly to allow the sugar to dissolve, then boil hard for 4 minutes only. Remove from the heat, skim any scum from the surface and stir in the violet essence to taste. I used about half of my precious 15 ml phial. Decant the jelly into clean, dry, hot jars, seal and label.

makes about 4 x 200 g jars

1 large Bramley apple
1 bunch red or black grapes
    about 750 g–1 kg/1½–2 lb
1 tablespoon lemon juice
preserving sugar – see recipe
violet syrup (p.32)
violet essence

Cook's tip

Although the essence stands up to cooking without losing its flavour, it is essential that you do not add it before skimming the surface or the oil will float to the top and mix with the foam, so that much of the essence is removed when you skim the surface.

Violet ice-cream

The basis of this beautiful dessert is the violet jelly described in the previous recipe. Serve it with crisp almond biscuits or as part of a trio with rose petal and chocolate ice-cream to mirror the flavour of old-fashioned chocolates filled with rose and violet cream.

Put the cream in a saucepan, bring just to the boil and pour it over the egg yolks, stirring all the time. Pour the mixture back into the rinsed saucepan and cook very gently just until the mixture thickens but does not curdle. If you prefer, you can cook the custard in a double boiler or bain marie. Once thickened, strain into a bowl. Gently melt the violet jelly and mix it thoroughly with the custard. Allow to cool, then pour into an ice-cream maker and freeze. Crystallised violets will decorate this very nicely.

serves 4 to 6

This recipe uses uncooked eggs

600 ml / 20 fl oz single cream
4 or 5 egg yolks, lightly beaten
1 x 200 g / 7 oz jar violet jelly

Spring violet cake

Using a lemon flavour, with lemon yellow or pale violet water icing, crystallised violets or frosted fresh flowers and a filling of cream and lemon curd, this makes an exquisite cake for a special spring tea party. As well as violets, frosted acacia flowers and primroses would look very pretty – see p.36. The recipe is the classic English sponge cake, moist and light, with good keeping qualities.

Cream the butter and sugar thoroughly until pale, light and fluffy. Lightly beat the eggs, then gradually incorporate them, a little at a time, alternating with a spoonful of flour, into the creamed mixture, together with the lemon zest and juice. Gently fold in the flour once the eggs have been incorporated.

Spoon the batter into two 20 cm/8 inch greased and floured sandwich tins, smooth the top and bake for 20 to 25 minutes in an oven pre-heated to 180°C/350°F/gas mark 4.

serves 8

175 g / 6 oz unsalted butter
175 g / 6 oz golden caster sugar
3 large eggs
finely pared zest of 2 lemons
juice of 1 lemon
175 g / 6 oz self-raising flour, sifted

Decoration
lemon curd
icing sugar
violet syrup or food colouring
water
crystallised violets or frosted fresh flowers

Allow to cool in the tin for a few minutes and then ease out the sponges to cool on wire racks.

To serve, sandwich with lemon curd and cover with violet water icing. To make the icing, sift icing sugar into a bowl and stir in no more than a drop of violet syrup or food colouring. Add just sufficient water to make a spreading consistency. Smooth it all over the cake, including the sides and, just before it has set, arrange the decorations on top of the cake.

Cook's tip

The cake can be baked the day before required and kept in an airtight container once cool. Alternatively, you can make the cake in advance. Wrap the two halves and freeze them. Cakes of this type freeze well.

Violet soufflé

This recipe relies on ingredients from your store cupboard rather than a foray to gather fresh violets. It is a spectacular dessert.

Melt the butter and stir in the flour, cooking the mixture for a few minutes without letting it colour. Remove from the heat and add a little hot milk. Stir until smooth, then – with the pan back on the heat again – gradually add the rest of the milk, stirring continuously to ensure a lump-free mixture. Cook for two or three minutes and remove from the heat. Lightly beat the egg yolks and stir them into the béchamel, together with the sugar. Whisk the egg whites to firm peaks, then, before you fold them with a metal spoon into the egg yolk mixture, add the crushed violets, the essence and the syrup to the soufflé mixture.

Spoon into a greased 1 litre/2 pint soufflé dish, place on a baking sheet and bake for 22 minutes in an oven pre-heated to 180°C/350°F/gas mark 4. Use the extra crystallised violets to decorate the soufflé before serving.

serves 4 to 6

25 g / 1 oz unsalted butter
1 tablespoon plain flour
300 ml / ½ pint rice milk or
    semi-skimmed milk
4 eggs, separated
1 oz / 25 g violet sugar or
    caster sugar
1 oz / 25 g crystallised violets,
    crushed, plus 5 extra for
    decoration
a drop of violet essence (p.44)
½ teaspoon violet syrup (p.32)

Pansies

Pansies, violas and heartsease, known by Shakespeare as Love-in-idleness and in North America as Johnny Jump Up, have for centuries been used to make syrups for sore throats and chest infections. These syrups can today be turned into delicious desserts and ice-creams.

Not as fragrant as violets, pansies have only a very faint scent, but the colour obtained in a pansy syrup is so pretty that it is worth the trouble of harvesting a few of these good-tempered garden flowers. Choose the very darkest purple blooms, even those called black pansies, rather than the red, yellow or multi-coloured varieties, and use the syrup recipe on p.32. With this as a base, you can also make a pansy sorbet or ice-cream, or adapt the violet spring cake on p.206 and decorate it with frosted heartsease or pansy flowers.

Salmon salad with purple potatoes, violet asparagus and pansies

Some years ago I prepared a feature for *Victoria* magazine involving a photo shoot at the Mark Hotel in Manhattan. The chef and I produced all manner of high-tea dishes, one of which was a fresh salmon salad, although it was quite unlike any salmon salad that ever appeared on our Sunday tea table when I was a child! It does depend, of course, on being able to find purple potatoes, violet asparagus and purple pansies at the same time. The rest is easy, and hardly requires a recipe.

Scrub and boil the potatoes. Allow them to cool slightly and then halve them in order to get the full dramatic effect of their colour. Trim and then steam or boil the asparagus. Cut the salmon fillets into neat rectangles or lozenge shapes and cook them on the griddle, or on baking sheets in the oven if you are cooking a large quantity.

Assemble the salad on a platter or on individual plates, starting with a bed of salad leaves, then the salmon with the potatoes and asparagus around it, and a few purple pansy flowers for decoration. Make a vinaigrette with violet vinegar (p.35) and syrup (p.32), and a mild and fruity extra virgin olive oil rather than a peppery one. Spoon this over the vegetables and serve.

Pansy oil

Instead of the vinaigrette for the preceding recipe, try a violet or pansy oil, vivid and strikingly purple, just right for this dish, and also good with grilled chicken or roasted quails. I have never made it for long keeping, instead using it over a two-day period, as an oil the first day and as an addition to a mayonnaise the next.

makes 200 ml / 7 fl oz

25 g / 1 oz purple pansy petals
200 ml / 7 fl oz oil,
as suggested in the recipe

You need to use a neutral oil like grapeseed or sunflower. The colour and flavour of a good extra virgin olive oil is too distinctive. Untoasted groundnut oil (peanut oil) is also an excellent neutral oil.

Simply put the petals and oil in the blender and blend until homogenised. You can sieve the mixture or not, as you prefer. Pour into a glass jug and cover until required. Stir just before using.

A mixed bunch

This chapter is where I give recipes featuring flowers that have just one perfect use, perhaps two, but no other, for it is not my intention to pad out this book with entire chapters on day lilies, hibiscus, acacia, hollyhocks or gladioli, even though these are all edible flowers.

Nor do I wish to devote excessive space to herb flowers, whose use is, on the whole, pretty obvious. If basil is delicious on a tomato salad, so too are basil flowers. Sage flower fritters will, of course, be perfect with griddled calf's liver, and sage flower dumplings with a pork and cider casserole. Some of the herb flowers lend themselves to crystallising or frosting for use in sweet dishes. Again, this is fairly obvious – you might want to crystallise rosemary flowers to decorate a chocolate cake, but would not, I suspect, choose to crystallise chive or garlic flowers.

*'And I will make thee beds
    of Roses
A thousand fragrant posies,
A cap of Flowers and a kirtle
Embroidered all with leaves
    of Myrtle.'*

Christopher Marlowe
The Passionate Shepherd to his Love

Acacia, mimosa

More than once when walking towards my local florist on a grey winter's day, I have been stopped in my tracks by the unmistakeable but almost indescribable scent of acacia blossoms. A few puffy yellow balls on a slim stem, the rest of the flowers in tight buds as tiny as peppercorns, the flat, silvery leaves – these speak of spring and sun and Mediterranean warmth. And who, in London in January, would not want to capture that in the kitchen?

The flavour is so fleeting, however, that the best way to use them in the kitchen is to crystallise or frost the flowers and serve them as a sweetmeat, a cake decoration or a garnish for desserts – see the methods give on p.37.

Common or false acacia, *Robinia pseudoacacia*, a member of the *Leguminosae* family with fragrant bunches of pretty pale cream flowers, is a common tree in parks and urban areas. I have been served them in salads in Italy and come across references to their use in fritters in France and in fragrant preserves in the Balkans. Geoffrey Grigson described the fritters as 'good – though a trifle *loosening*', but my bible on such matters, *Poisonous Plants and Fungi*, states that **all parts of this tree are poisonous.**

Alliums, garlic chives, wild garlic

These are deeply savoury and pungent flowers, ideally suited to flavouring egg, cheese, rice and pasta dishes, and some of them add a startling blue note that is especially effective when served with pale food. Try allium flowers stirred into and scattered on top of a pasta salad, bound with plenty of mayonnaise in a potato and shellfish salad or scattered onto a potato soup just before serving.

Wild or wood garlic, also known as ramsons, is sometimes sold during the spring in independent greengrocers and farmers' markets, and it can be found in the wild. It was a popular salad herb in Elizabethan England. I like to stir both leaves and flowers into a tomato risotto, finely shredding the former and leaving the flowers whole. They are also excellent combined with other spring vegetables in omelettes, flans and tarts. If you can obtain a large enough bunch, use it to make a flavoursome soup thickened with potatoes, or mix the chopped flowers and leaves with ricotta, nutmeg, a little Parmesan and some crushed and toasted hazelnuts to make an excellent stuffing for home-made ravioli.

Alliaria petiolata is not a member of the onion family, but has a slightly garlicky flavour and can be used in the same way as ramsons. Garlic mustard, Sauce-Alone and Jack-by-the-hedge are other names for this wild herb, which is usually found in shady places. It has pretty white flowers that can be mixed with the leaves or, if you use the leaves to make a sauce for wild salmon or new season's lamb, the flowers can be woven into a decorative wreath; make it as you used to make daisy chains, with one flower threaded through a slit in the stem of another.

Bergamot, oswego

This bergamot (*Monarda didyma*) is a herb originally from North America, where it is also known as bee-weed. It has nothing to do with the oil of bergamot used to scent Earl Grey tea, which is extracted from the peel of a member of the citrus family of the same name. The bright red flowers are used to make Oswego tea, prepared like any other tisane, and it also makes an attractive addition to flower confetti (see p.38).

Camomile

Its sweet, hay-like fragrance and bitter flavour make camomile an acquired taste. I like it for tisanes, cordials and sorbets – the latter is particularly delicious after the cheese course and before dessert – but do not feel that it lends itself to a whole array of delicate creams, custards and other puddings. Those who disagree will prove me wrong, I am sure.

Spring brings with it carpets of wild camomile, also known as mayweed, on the island of Gozo, where it has been used for generations to make a herbal infusion and also in poultices as a specific against stomach ache.

Camomile sorbet

Thinly peel off the lime zest, put it in a jug with the camomile, pour on the boiling water and leave to infuse for 10 minutes. Stir in the juice from the limes and the sugar, then, when the latter has dissolved, strain the infusion, cool and freeze. Using the lesser amount of sugar will give you a grainier sorbet, while more sugar will make it smoother.

serves 6

2 limes
2–3 tablespoons dried camomile
   flowers
600 ml/1 pint water
300–400 g/10–14 oz
   granulated sugar

Chrysanthemum

Dried chrysanthemum petals are used in both Japanese and Chinese clear soups, and can be very decorative. Their flavour is mildly peppery, but the fragrance is fleeting and not one to be extracted into syrups, butters, etc. A chrysanthemum vinegar would look very attractive in the bottle.

Clover

There are many traditional recipes for a wine made with purple clover, and I have seen white clover flowers used in salads. Both varieties have an agreeable, if very mild, flavour and there is, of course, a taste of honey at the base of purple clover flowers. Wild flower meadows are increasingly scarce, however, and recipes involving clover are not really practical nowadays.

Cornflowers

These soft, ragged flowers offer one of the truest blues to be found in nature, and for that reason alone I love to include them in summer flower arrangements, preferably combined with lots of deep, clear yellow. The flowers are edible, but have little or no scent, as you will know if you have ever bought *eau de bleuet* as a skin freshener, and little flavour.

Despite their lack of scent, I include cornflowers here because they look so fabulous as part of a fresh flower confetti, mixed with other small or shredded petals, especially yellow, orange and white, and scattered over salads, omelettes, *frittate* and vegetable pasta dishes.

You can use the confetti as it is or turn it into a millefleur mayonnaise or millefleur hollandaise simply by folding the fresh petals carefully into your chosen sauce. Neither should be too vinegary, and the hollandaise should be warm rather than hot, otherwise the flowers will discolour and their brightness will be lost.

To use cornflowers in this way, simply separate the flower into its individual petals.

Courgette or zucchini flowers, squash blossoms

Visit almost any Mediterranean market in early summer and you will see heaps of golden trumpets, the delicate flowers removed from various members of the squash family. Occasionally they are sold still attached to the tiny vegetable, and traditionally they are cooked together, the flowers stuffed with rice, cheese and herbs and the whole placed in an oiled dish and baked in the oven. Increasingly, courgette flowers are to be found in farmers' markets in Britain and North America, and, of course, are one of the bonuses of growing your own vegetables. Both male and female flowers can be used.

They are fragile, so handle them carefully and use as soon as possible after picking. Shake off any insects, but try to avoid rinsing them. For the stuffing, mix cooked rice or couscous, some grated cheese, chopped herbs such as chervil or parsley and chives and, if you like, a few shreds of cured or cooked ham. Holding the blossom in one hand, carefully deposit a spoonful of the stuffing inside, then fold over the petals to enclose it. Put in an oiled dish and stuff all the blossoms in the same way. Spoon a little olive oil over them and bake at 180°C/350°F/gas mark 4 for about 20 minutes.

Cowslips

These delicate, nodding golden flowers are beautiful when in a wild flower meadow, but, despite the fact that early cookbooks give numerous recipes for cowslips – in wine, syrup, tea, cream, sugar, mead, even in cakes and puddings – I am not including any here, as they should be protected.

Dandelions

The dandelion, *Taraxacum officinale*, has a long history of pharmaceutical use, as there are many disorders for which the plant provides a cure. Liver, kidney and skin complaints are all said to benefit, as is rheumatism. Nowadays there is a good deal of interest in its health-giving properties, which arise from dandelions having unusually long roots that penetrate through the topsoil, which is relatively poor in nutrients compared with the subsoil, from where the plant draws in a variety of minerals and other substances.

Whilst dandelion leaves are the principal component of the classic French *salade de pissenlits*, the flowers have long been used in rural England to make wine. They can also be used to make an infusion, and thence into a syrup or jelly. I have come across more modern recipes calling for the flowers in bud to be dipped in batter and deep-fried, to be eaten as a snack, a first course or an accompaniment to fish or chicken.

Dandelion salad should only be made with the leaves of young plants that have yet to flower – those picked any later will be coarse and almost inedible. Walnut oil makes a delicious dressing for this overlooked leaf.

Day lilies

Orange, lemon yellow, egg-yolk yellow, deep red and variegated, these are strikingly attractive flowers, cultivated in British gardens but to be found in the wild in many parts of the United States.

In America, day lily buds are deep-fried and served as one would okra. I have also read suggestions for using the open flowers as a receptacle in which to serve a mousse or a flavoured cream cheese preparation as an appetiser. You can use open hollyhock flowers in the same way.

While they have no particular scent to extract, day lilies do have an agreeable taste and texture, reminiscent of young courgettes shaved into strips and eaten raw. They certainly add colour and texture to salads, either whole or divided into spear-shaped petals.

Note: these recommendations apply only to day lilies and not to the wide variety of hybrids, scented or otherwise.

Hibiscus, roselle

In Mexico, squash blossoms, linden and hibiscus flowers are all used in the kitchen; historically, the flower of the cocoa tree was used, as was that of the *mamey*, a large, round, rough-skinned fruit with something of the taste and texture of a mango. Hibiscus is called *jamaica* is Mexico, while in Jamaica a refreshing drink is made with hibiscus, which the islanders call sorrel. A similar drink, *karkadeeh*, is made in Egypt, comprising simply water, petals and sugar. You can use fresh or dried hibiscus and you will find that the flavour is tart, not unlike the sumac found in Middle Eastern cooking, or cranberries. In fact, it is the calyx of the flower that is used, after the petals have dropped off. Because they contain an appreciable amount of pectin, hibiscus flowers are also useful in making preserves and jellies.

To make a refreshing drink, steep the hibiscus flowers

in boiling water for 10 minutes, experimenting with quantities to get the depth of flavour you prefer. Strain and sweeten to taste. Cool, then chill before drinking.

To make a hibiscus sorbet, just add an equal volume of sugar to the infusion, which should be on the strong side. Chill and then freeze as usual.

Hyssop

The pale blue flowers of hyssop are every bit as pretty as rosemary flowers and, like them, are worth frosting to use as garnish – see p.37. The delicacy of the scent and flavour is such that you would need far too many to flavour a cream or butter by *enfleurage*, or a sugar by simply keeping some flowers in a jar of sugar, but you could blend flowers with butter or cream, or grind them with sugar.

Lilac

Immensely fragrant on the tree, especially after a spring shower, lilac has the most fleeting of perfumes and I have never managed to capture this in a cream, sugar, vinegar or other preparation. Perhaps others may be more fortunate, following any of the methods given in this book. Failing all else, the flowers can be used fresh to decorate a salad or frosted to use on a cake or dessert.

Myrtle

This attractive evergreen bush is a useful plant for the herb garden, and its small shiny leaves can be employed as you would bay leaves. They have a not dissimilar aroma, but a slightly sweeter perfume. The berries have a flavour akin to juniper, to which myrtle is related, and can be used in similar ways, although a gin distiller might disagree with me. Myrtle flowers are small, pretty, white tinged with pink, not unlike hawthorn blossom, but with a fresher, sweeter scent, not as musky as the hawthorn.

The flowers make a nice addition to a floral salad decoration, perhaps with elderflower and strawberry flowers, hawthorn flowers and white lilac, separated from all the green parts.

Myrtle flowers are distilled to make the classic *eau d'ange*, which is used to perfume soaps and other cosmetics, and are also used in *crème de laurier*, a brandy-based ratafia, which includes bay leaves (*laurier* in French). I have seen this recipe on several websites on which *laurier* is translated as laurel. This is both wrong and dangerous: **laurel leaves are poisonous**. But using myrtle flowers and bay leaves, you might like to have a go.

Crème de laurier

Bruise the spices, flowers and leaves in a mortar, put them in a wide-necked jar or decanter and pour over the brandy, or simply whiz in the blender with the brandy. Cork and leave to infuse for 5 days. Make a syrup with the sugar and about 50 ml / 2 fl oz water. Mix with the infused brandy, strain through fine muslin or sieve, then bottle and label.

1 nutmeg, coarsely grated
6 cloves
25 g / 1 oz myrtle flowers
35 g / 1½ oz bay leaves
5 tablespoons brandy
300 g / 10 oz sugar

Pea

The white flower of the garden pea is pleasant, slightly sweet and, surprisingly enough, tastes like the pea. Of course, if you eat all your pea flowers you will have no peas to harvest, but for a special summer salad decorated with edible white flowers, very pretty against baby spinach and other dark green leaves, it is worth using a few pea flowers. I would dress such a salad with a sweet vinegar, such as raspberry, and hazelnut, walnut or roasted peanut oil.

Important note: I refer here to the garden pea, not to the flowering sweet pea, which is toxic.

Primrose

Along with its relative the cowslip, the primrose has
long been used in country recipes, in conserves and to
make a richly flavoured golden wine. Its planting in
'the kitchen garden' was suggested as early as the
sixteenth century, and much later the flowers were
recommended as a garnish for a sweet and spicy
latticed parsnip pie, served cold. The scent of the fresh
flower is delightful, sweet, rose-like and delicate.
I think you would need far too many of them to
make creams or sugars with them. Use a handful to
frost and decorate a spring cake or tart, but if you
want more, then plant your own primrose path.

Sweet cicely

With the same sweet anis flavour as its feathery leaves,
this lacy flower is an agreeable addition to flower-
strewn salads and by following the instructions on
p.37 you can also frost the flowers, which make an
ideal decoration for a fruit flan.

A glassful of flowers

Flower cocktails

Once you have made your own flower syrups and ratafias, you will soon realise how useful they are for perfuming fruit salads, spooning over sorbets or ice-creams and flavouring chicken casseroles, and they will rapidly become every bit as useful as bottles of Tabasco and Angostura bitters. And the cocktails you can make with them are fabulous! Imagine a frozen rose petal daiquiri, an elderflower martini, a violet margarita. All these – and many more – are possible: the only limit is your imagination.

I prefer to use a white spirit – rum, gin, vodka, tequila – primarily for aesthetic reasons, as a darker spirit distorts the colour of the cocktail. But on the other hand, an aged rum, saffron syrup, a dash of Grand Marnier, the juice of a bitter orange – there are distinct possibilities there.

On different occasions I have used pink grapefruit juice, strained passion fruit juice and juice from freshly squeezed limes, lemons or Seville oranges for the 'sour'. The best flower cocktails are made with complementary flavours and similar colours.

True *aficionados* will have a whole panoply of liqueurs and spirits with which to enhance their drinks, a trickle of Galliano here, a drop or two of Aperol there.

A real *barista* would almost certainly want to add a drop of Sambucca to the elderflower margarita, but in the recipes that follow I have restricted myself to easily available components.

Here I simply give a few of my favourite recipes to help get you started. A cocktail shaker, although not *de rigueur*, is very useful, and it is also well worth chilling the glasses in the freezer beforehand. Each recipe serves one.

Rosa cubana

This is based on the Mojito, with white rum and mint being the key ingredients.

Put the mint and plenty of ice cubes in a cocktail shaker or glass jug. Bruise the mint against the ice cubes and then add the rest of the ingredients. Stir vigorously to chill the liquids, then strain into a glass and add the sprig of mint and rose petals before serving.

1 stalk of fresh mint, plus 1 small sprig for garnish
ice cubes
1 measure rose petal syrup (p.32)
1 measure white rum
1–2 measures pink grapefruit juice
rose petals – optional

Tropical rose

The pink-fleshed guava and the translucent lychee are both reminiscent of roses, and their juices combined with rose petal syrup make a heavenly cocktail, the sharp note of lime juice preventing it from being too cloying.

Shake all the ingredients over ice and pour into a chilled glass with a couple of rose petals floated on top.

1 measure guava juice
1 measure lychee juice
1 measure rose petal syrup (p.32)
1 measure fresh lime juice
1 measure white rum
rose petals to garnish

Frozen elderflower margarita

For this you need a sturdy blender, and it is worth making two or three at the same time.

Put all the ingredients in the blender and set it on the lowest speed for 10 to 15 seconds to crush the ice cubes, then blend until you have a frozen homogeneous mass. Transfer to chilled cocktail glasses.

9 large ice cubes
juice of 3 limes
3 measures white tequila
1 measure Cointreau
3 measures elderflower cordial
(p.59)

Turkish delightini

The range of martinis on offer in bars is seemingly endless. Here is another, in which the rose and lemon taste just as in the toothsome sweetmeat.

Wet the rim of the martini glass and dip it in the powdered icing sugar. Stir or shake the remaining ingredients, at length, over plenty of ice and strain into the prepared glass. Splash or spray a little rosewater over the surface before serving to obtain the authentic sweet Turkish Delight experience.

icing sugar (powdered)
1 measure rose petal syrup (p.32)
1 measure freshly squeezed lemon juice
2 measures gin or vodka
rosewater

Elderflower martini

Using Plymouth gin rather than vodka, this, for me, is a quintessential English summer drink.

Stir the ingredients over plenty of ice and strain into a cocktail glass.

For a long drink, gin with a splash of elderflower cordial and plenty of chilled sparkling mineral water makes a drink far superior to gin and tonic.

1 1/2 measures Plymouth gin
1/2 measure elderflower cordial (p.59)
juice of half a lime or lemon

Parfait amour

This is my own version of a classic cocktail, which you can make with the *sirop de violette* from Toulouse.

Stir all the ingredients over ice and strain into a chilled glass.

1 measure crème de cassis
1 measure vodka
1 measure still mineral water
1 teaspoon violet syrup (p.32)
juice of half a lime

Lavender julep

I make this with bourbon, following the method for the classic mint julep, but it is also very good with export-strength Plymouth gin, although it then ceases to be a julep. It is, of course, best if the bottle of bourbon or other spirit is kept in the freezer.

Put the lavender stalk in the tumbler, head down and muddle or crush it with the sugar, adding the water as you do so. Fill the tumbler with ice and pour the bourbon over the top. Use the stalk to stir it with the ice, then top with a sprig of lavender and serve.

1 very fresh, long, sturdy
   lavender stalk
1 tablespoon sugar
1 measure water
crushed ice, sufficient to fill the
   tumbler
1–1½ measures bourbon
sprig of fresh lavender for garnish

Flowers and wine

Flower desserts and sweet wines make a very happy marriage at the end of a meal and it is always worth hunting out an unusual bottle or half-bottle. Muscat de Beaumes de Venise and other sweet muscats, Mauzac Nature, a *méthode gaillacoise* from the Languedoc and Cerdon du Bugey, *demi-sec* and very flowery-grapey, are all good with pastry, cake and batter desserts flavoured with flowers, for example, the elderflower tart on p.66 or the rose petal kulfi on p.176.

Vin de paille from France and Schilfwein from Austria both have the concentrated honey flavour that comes from ripe grapes being laid on mats to dry in the sun and are excellent with the saffron-scented desserts on pages 187–9.

With desserts containing berry fruit or citrus as well as a flower flavour, I recommend sweet Loire wines or late-harvest riesling or other German/Alsatian varietals, whether from Australia, Austria, California, England or Canada, and the chenin-based white wines of South Africa. These have enough acidity to balance that in the fruit. The gooseberry and elderflower crumble on p.63 served with a Bonnezaux, for example, is a marriage made in heaven.

In certain wines, distinctive flower notes can be detected, of which the classic example is gewürztraminer, with its hints of lychees and roses.

A *vendange tardive* or *sélection de grains nobles*, would be truly exquisite with the rose-flavoured dessert recipes on pages 169–77. A *grand cru* gewürztraminer, less sweet, but very fragrant, could accompany the chicken, almond and rose pudding on p.178, but with that you might also try a very fine mature red Burgundy, which unfurls to reveal roses on the nose as well as very delicate spice notes.

Dishes using elderflower and hawthorn should be tried not only with wines made from the sauvignon blanc grape, whether from New Zealand or the Touraine, but also with English white wines, which are so delightfully reminiscent of English hedgerows. When using elderflower in a dessert however, you cannot go wrong if you serve it with a Muscat wine, preferably an unfortified one. This will be a better partner for the subtlety of the flowers than one with a heavier dose of alcohol. Chasselas, which also has a frank, grapey nose, is worth experimenting with, especially paired with savoury dishes using elderflowers.

While it is true that Chinon and Bourgueil, Loire reds made from the cabernet franc grape, often reveal a nose with hints of violets, that flavour is too subtle to pair with a red wine. In any case, my violet-flavoured dishes are generally sweet, for which red wines are a poor partner, with a few exceptions like matching chocolate desserts with the wines of Banyuls or Maury from south-western France.

With violet-scented desserts, I would opt for a sweet German wine, a Spätlese or an Auslese. They are both low in alcohol, so will not overpower the very delicate flower scent. As a match for the salmon recipe on p.208, with its delicate pansy accompaniments, try a Condrieu or another wine made from the viognier grape, which is notable for its soft, floral nose.

Given that gewürztraminer means 'spicy', clove pinks, with their spicy scent, are well partnered by this distinctive Alsace wine. But if that is too powerful for you (and I must admit that it is not a wine I drink very often), I would recommend another white from the same region, pinot gris, which is also known as tokay d'Alsace.

What wine to serve with lavender has been the subject of lengthy and enjoyable research. It is, with the rose, the most distinctive of the flower scents and the flavour carries through into the dish in a very pure form. As a partner to sweet lavender recipes I find that the more acidic sweet wines, such as those from the Loire and the Mosel, are more appropriate than the honeyed wines of the south-west, the Monbazillac and Loupiacs, the Sauternes and Barsacs. However, Maury and Banyuls, red wines both, are the wines I recommend with the chocolate and lavender desserts on pages 104 and 105.

With fish or pale meat dishes using lavender, a semillon/sauvignon blend such as you will find in a dry white Bordeaux makes an interesting partnership. With a red meat, I prefer a tannic wine, which will match the power of the lavender oil that carries the flavour; try a Chianti or a Barbera, for example.

Index